DURAN DURAN, IMELDA MARCOS, AND ME

A GRAPHIC MEMOIR BY
LORINA MAPA

First Edition
ISBN 978-177262-011-5

Printed by Gauvin in Gatineau, Quebec

Conundrum Press
Wolfville, Nova Scotia, Canada
www.conundrumpress.com

Distributed in Canada by Litdistco
Distributed in UK by Turnaround
Distributed in US by Consortium

Conundrum Press acknowledges the financial support of the
Canada Council for the Arts, the government of Canada through
the Canada Book Fund, and the Province of Nova Scotia's Creative
Industries Fund toward its publishing activities.

Canada Council
for the Arts

Conseil des Arts
du Canada

DURAN DURAN, IMELDA MARCOS, AND ME

A GRAPHIC MEMOIR BY LORINA MAPA

March 3, 2005. It is 7:00 in the evening. I've just had an ultrasound at Dr. Mercier's office and am at my sister-in-law Sandra's house to pick up my nephew Kristofer for a sleepover.

DING DONG

Hi, Rina. Daniel was just on the phone and said to call him back as soon as you got here. He sounded very serious.

?

Hey Babe! What's up?

I've been trying the cellphone for the past hour but I couldn't reach you.

The battery died on my way to Dr. Mercier's. Why? What's wrong?

Rina...you need to come home right now. Don't bring Kristofer.

Why? What's happened?

Hello?

Babe?

Your dad's been in a car accident.

WHAT?! OH MY GOD, HOW IS HE?? IS HE OKAY??

Just come home.

What's wrong??

1

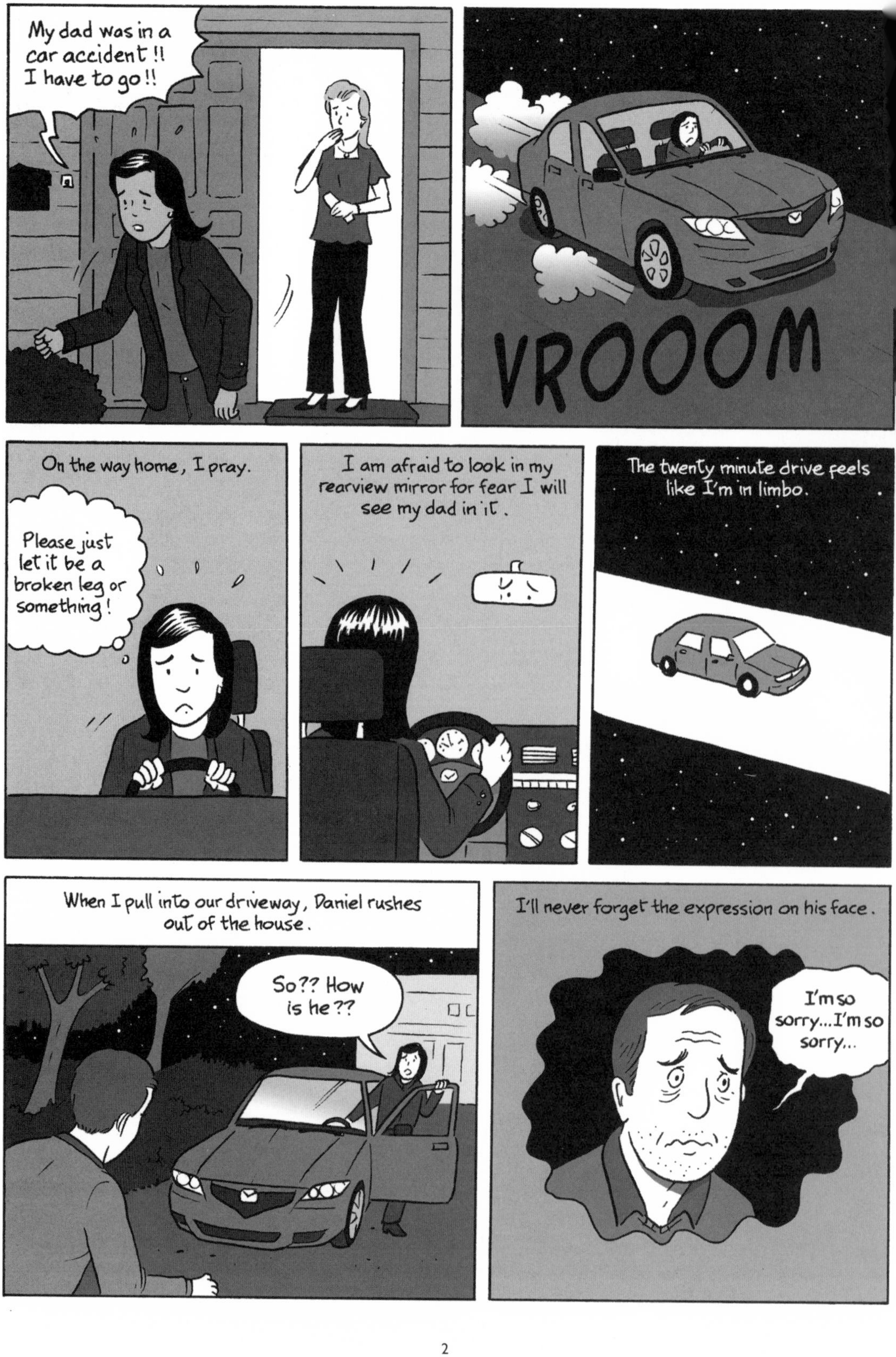
My dad was in a car accident !! I have to go !!
VROOOM
On the way home, I pray.
Please just let it be a broken leg or something !
I am afraid to look in my rearview mirror for fear I will see my dad in it.
The twenty minute drive feels like I'm in limbo.
When I pull into our driveway, Daniel rushes out of the house.
So?? How is he??
I'll never forget the expression on his face.
I'm so sorry...I'm so sorry...

NOOOOOOOO!!!

My three boys, Michael, Alec and Nicholas, are waiting for me in the kitchen.

Three-year-old Alec is very sensitive to what's going on.

Mommy? Why are you crying?

Having to comfort him helps me keep it together.

I'm okay, sweetie.

When...? How...?

Early morning, their time. A sugar cane truck with busted headlights hit his car.

The rest of my family live in the Philippines, which has a 12-hour time difference. My dad was traveling early for work, and the accident happened at 4:00 am, o a remote country road in Negros, San Carlos, about 900 km south of Manila.

But are you *sure* he's dead?? *How sure* are they?? I mean, how'd you find out...?

Nini called.

Tito Tony has died in a car accident!!!

OMG Tito Tony! NOOO!!!

Tito Tony was just in a car accident. he's dead

Does Rina know?

Within hours, a network of relatives and friends living all over the world was texting each other, from New Zealand to London, from San Francisco to Washington DC. In New York, my cousin Nini confirmed it was fatal before breaking the news to Daniel. So I am actually one of the last ones to find out.

The phone has been ringing non-stop. I have no desire to talk to anyone. What I want is to go to bed and pretend none of this is happening. I'm such a coward that I'm even afraid to call my mom, afraid of how I will react.

I can't, Babe.

But Daniel insists I take every single call. He doesn't really give me a choice, even though I just want to be left alone. And everyone turns out to be so gentle and sympathetic that afterwards, I feel brave enough to call my mom.

She sounds groggy and medicated. Even now I ask, "But are you *SURE* he's dead? *HOW SURE* are you?"

My mom is patient, not frustrated with my denial. In the saddest voice I've ever heard she says, "It's sure, Rin." She tells me my older brother Tonton flew out to identify my dad's broken body and is bringing him home to Manila for burial. I grow silent, shamed by guilt, thinking of what Ton must be going through.

Daniel has arranged for the three of us (including our eldest son Nicholas) to fly to Manila the next day while his parents look after Michael and Alec. Finally we go to bed.

But of course I can't sleep. Memories that had faded with the passage of time come rushing back with a strange clarity, the way sometimes when you dream in the early morning, you are aware you are dreaming, but the dream feels infinitely more real than being awake.

Hi, Princess...

Do you want to help me wash the car?

YA!

My dad called me "Princess" almost from the moment I was born.

I was an ugly baby with a boxer's face, the first girl after a handsome older brother with delicate features.

Happily this ugly stage was temporary, although the nickname "Princess" was not.

Even as I grew older and went through a very long period where I rejected party dresses and sandals for jeans and sneakers, I was always "Princess" to my dad.

Please, Rina! It's *tita** Peachy's wedding, and you're the flower girl!

NOOOO!

*aunt

You are wearing this dress whether you like it or not!

Wedding of Peachy and Orly Trias, 1975

PEACHY

ORLY

ME

GOODY TWO-SHOES BOY

I ended up ruining all the pictures I was in with this expression. Sadly for Peachy, there was no Photoshop back then.

When I was six years old, my sister Lisa was born, the fourth child after my brother Nikko.

Hello, sweet little princess.

Hey! I thought *I* was your Princess!

Of course you are! You are, ah, my ORIGINAL princess!

What's "original" mean?

It means the first... and still the best!

Oh! Okay, then.

On birthday cards to my dad, I made sure to sign them "OP" (Original Princess) so he wouldn't forget.

This struck him as funny and he forever referred to me as "O.P." in his own letters afterwards.

Eventually he gave different nicknames to Lisa ("Svettie") and my littlest sister Miel ("Mule") and was free to call me "Princess" again.

THE FIVE OF US
CIRCA 1979

TONTON (age 12) "MANONG"   RINA (9) "PRINCESS"   NIKKO (7) "KONGKOY"   LISA (3) "SVETTIE"   MIEL (2) "MULE"

He also called me "Bunny" because I loved rabbits and my two front teeth stuck out. On his trips to Europe he would bring back little rabbit souvenirs for me.

One day we were at the mall, looking for new *tsinelas.* My mom pointed out various options, all of them pink or with floral patterns.

How about these?

* flip-flops

Don't they have *tsinelas* with dogs or something?

I was also obsessed with dogs

Then I saw a pair I liked.

This one! Can I get this please?

Ha ha! With rabbits, huh? Sure, why not?

But Tony! They're for boys! And besides...

It's the Play boy Bunny!

She doesn't know what that means.

But what will people think?

So?

I happily wore my new *tsinelas* everyday when I came home from school. I was around ten at the time and only found out what those bunny icons really meant many years later. I think my dad was touched by my innocence.

From birth till the age of about 6 or 7, I lived in a big house with a beautiful garden.

We had a guava tree in which I would climb every day to wait for my older brother Tonton to arrive home from school.

I was three years younger and would wear one of his school uniforms while waiting for him. Tonton was very possessive of "his" tree and as soon as he got home he would insist I leave.

My older brother was brilliant and intense. I idolized him and constantly tried to imitate him.

From wanting to build model tanks and planes...

...To buying the same red Adidas running shoes.

Far from being amused, this annoyed Tonton no end. Like all little sisters, I worshipped my older brother in ways that were sneakily passive-aggressive.

Unfortunately for Ton, my dad usually indulged my desires with a smile.

Here, Princess, a Spitfire for you to try.

Tonton was fascinated by anything to do with World War II. In the manner of older brothers, he often tried to shock me with graphic and violent pictures from my dad's collection of Timelife books.

See, these soldiers were decapitated by a bayonet.

We'd huddle together in a leather bean bag in the den and look at these books for hours.

This guy was obviously killed by a grenade.

WW II

I remember a painting of a young soldier. Half of his body had been blown away by a bomb.

I looked at it often, both disturbed and fascinated by the expression of terror on his face and the half that was nothing but bloody cartilage.

I loved that den. It was always dark and cool, even during the hottest summer months. The walls were lined with shelves full of trophies from car rallies my dad had won over the years, and of course lots of books. When I read there, I really felt transported to another world.

While Tonton was in school, my little brother Nikko and I loved to play a game we invented called "Me! Me!"

We would look at coffeetable books such as "Animals of the Modern Kingdom" and take turns pointing to each picture, saying:

Me!

Me!

While some pictures were boring, like zebras grazing or a panda placidly chewing on a bamboo shoot, most were pretty entertaining.

EEEEK!! Me!

The Spicebush Swallowtail Caterpillar is one of the best mimics known.

THE GUINNESS B

WHOA! Me!

Jo-Jo the "Dog-Faced" Boy

Ripley's — Believe It

Me!

No, that's both of us!

Chang and Eng were the most famous conjoined Siamese twin

NATIONAL GEOGRAP

HA HA! Me!

Look at his butt!

An explorer taking an outdoor shower in the Arctic was a source of glee for days after.

11

On Friday nights, my dad would have his friends over for poker. They'd gather in the den with their cigarettes and Johnnie Walker whiskey, listening to Frank Sinatra crooning in the background.

Tito* Johnny Antillon, a jolly, generous man with an infectious laugh and a love for brandy.

Tito Dave and his dry, witty sense of humour, an intellectual, and very tall.

Tito Vince, friendly and always making little jokes.

Tito Ditos, who loved Placido Domingo and peanuts and smelled of cigarettes and cologne. He was very affectionate and let me sit on his lap and look at his cards.

Think I'll win this round?

Inday* Rina, time to sleep na.

Already?

You heard yaya* Luz.

Good night, Daddy.

'Night, Princess. Sweet dreams.

* Uncle   * Miss   * Nanny

12

Reluctantly, I'd go off to bed.

HA HA HA!

I left my bedroom door open so I could fall asleep to the sounds of clinking poker chips and men's deep, boisterous laughter, which made me feel very safe.

36 HOURS LATER...

We are now arriving at Ninoy Aquino International Airport.

Philippines

Please fasten your seatbelts. Thank you for flying Philippine Airlines. Mabuhay!

Phil. Jewelry & Gifts

KOFF KOFF

Handicraf TESORO'S

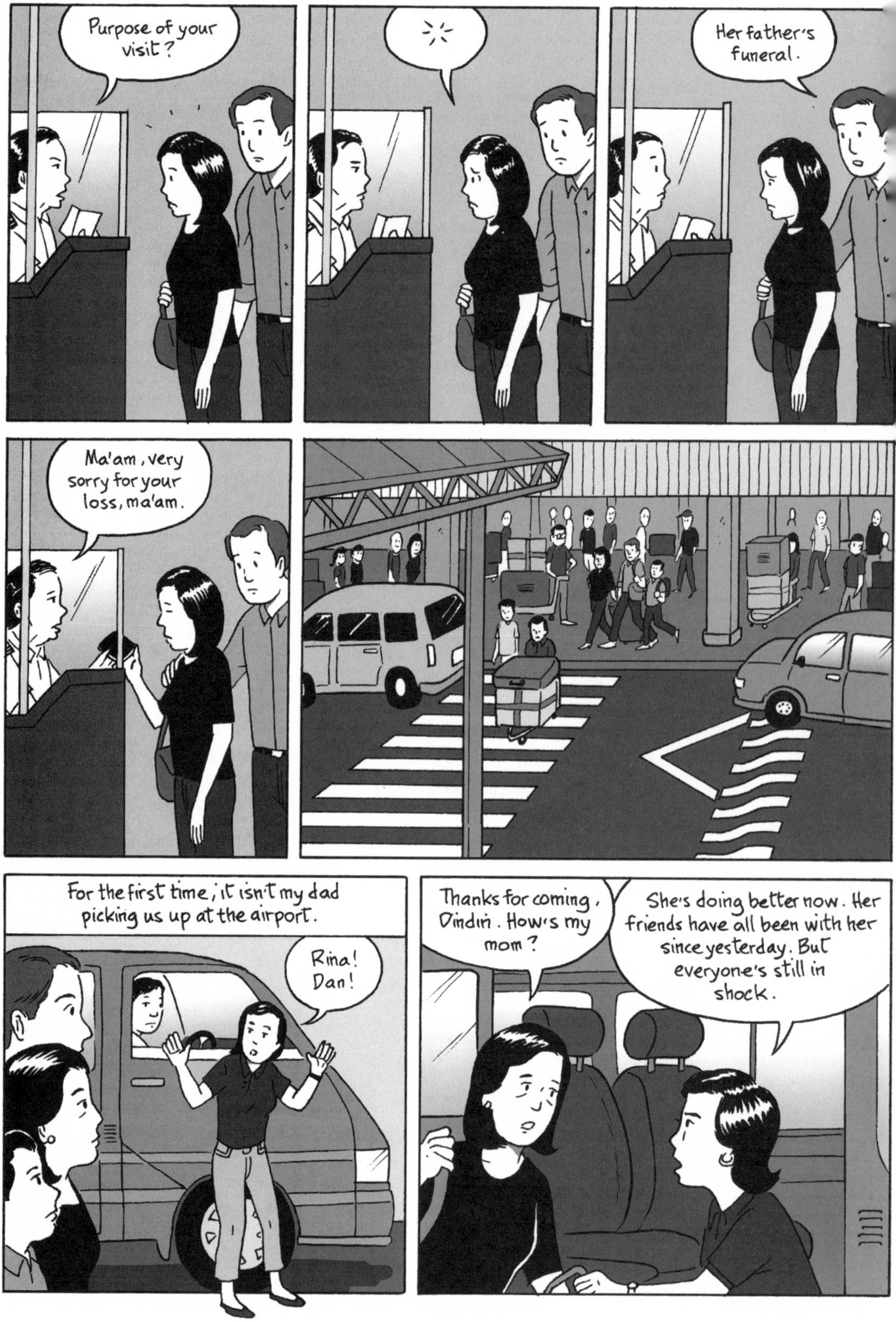

Purpose of your visit?
Her father's funeral.
Ma'am, very sorry for your loss, ma'am.
For the first time, it isn't my dad picking us up at the airport.
Rina! Dan!
Thanks for coming, Dindin. How's my mom?
She's doing better now. Her friends have all been with her since yesterday. But everyone's still in shock.

Here we are, Princess.

My *lola** lived in an exclusive gated community in Manila. Its main avenue was impressively lined with huge acacia trees.

As with other gated communities in parts of the Philippines, the guards would only let you enter if you were a resident with a special sticker, or a resident's guest.

*Grandmother

Crowds of poor people gathered outside the gates to beg or sell things to those who were driving into Forbes. Whenever our car was waiting by the traffic light at the entrance, we were besieged by street kids.

I wondered why so many were blind.

Please give just one peso.

≷TSK!≷ Sometimes it's actually inflicted by the one who is in charge of them so that people will feel sorry for them and give them money.

My *lola* kept a basket of individually packaged snacks in her car. She gave these to the beggar children instead of money.

They just take the money and give it to their boss, or else buy cigarettes and drugs.

This way, at least I can still help them.

16

Usually, the street urchins were pleased with the food.

Salamat, 'po.

But once a teenage boy was so insulted that he threw a package of crackers back at my *lola* and cursed her.

Putang ina!

Every Sunday, before having lunch with my mom's side of the family, we would hear mass at San Antonio church in Forbes Park.

Outside of the church, always at the same spot, was a man with no legs. His hair was neatly combed. He wore glasses and a formal dress shirt which was old and worn but very clean. Unlike the other beggars, he never approached anyone but sat on his makeshift platform on wheels with an angry, defeated look in his eyes.

He was squat and bulky, with powerful arms and no neck. I tried not to stare at him whenever I walked by.

I felt guilty all the time. Why him and not me?

Half an hour later, we'd arrive at my grandfather's house. The first thing I'd see when we came in was this sign hanging in the front hall.

I complained that I had no shoes until I saw a man who had no feet.

I found this extremely disturbing and morbid, especially after the man in church.

I had nightmares of my feet being hacked off in a freak accident if I so much as complained about anything.

No...

AAAAAAA AA!!

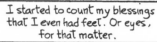

I started to count my blessings that I even had feet. Or eyes, for that matter.

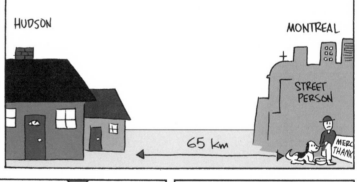

My children suffer from no such guilt, having spent all their lives in a picturesque and relatively affluent neighbourhood in Canada, miles away from the nearest street person.

HUDSON

MONTREAL

STREET PERSON

65 km

MERC THANK

Why do I have to walk half a kilometer to the bus stop when you can just drive me? What is the point of having a car, then?

It's always me who walks Nelly! I just walked her yesterday! Why did we even get a dog?

Hockey practice again? That's twice this week! Why can't I just go when it's a game? Dumb hockey!

In those moments, they are convinced they are the most unfortunate souls on earth, and I feel I have failed as a parent.

WHY YO... BUNCH OF UNG... DON'T YOU REALIZE HOW... LUCKY YOU ARE ?? HOW DARE YO... EVEN THINK ABOUT COMPLAIN

There's Lola!

Hi, Lola!

Thanks for the ride, Dindin.

Hi Nicholas! You sure have grown since the last time I saw you!

Thank you for coming, Dan. I know you're quite sick with pneumonia, no?

Rin...

≷SNIFF≷ So, come in, come in. How was your flight? How are you feeling? You hardly show.

You want to rest first or go see Dad?

I want to see Daddy.

Are you sure, Rin? Maybe you should eat something first. Don't forget you're eating for two!

See, here's some soup and *pancit** from tita Med.

Well... okay.

* noodles

Dindin told me that when my mom heard the news, she collapsed from high blood pressure and had to be medicated by paramedics.

So you're sure you're okay? No nausea? No air sickness?

I'm fine.

Now I see her distracting herself by worrying about others and chattering away.

The wake is being held at Manila Memorial, you remember that's where *lola* Loring and *lolo* Nene are buried, no?

In times of crisis she has always been able to hold it together.

MANILA MEMORIAL PARK

The phone has been ringing non-stop. And you should've seen all the people yesterday. The place was packed!

So many people! The Rachos, the Javellanas, the Hidalgos... of course, the Arcenas family...

Everyone was crying. As in everyone! Even *tito* Dave! And your cousins! My gosh, you'd think their own fathers had died.

Look at how many flowers for dad.

The hallway was so full we even donated some to the chapel here.

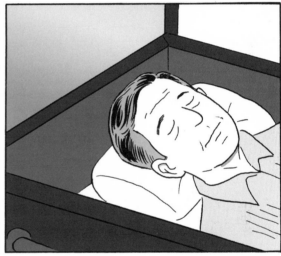

He really is dead!

It's a shock when you see him for the first time, no?

I'm not really sure what I was hoping for.

My dad loved surprises.

Hee hee hee!

AAAH!!

!

It's only me! Heh heh...

Uh, Daddy? I think Nikko peed.

Sometimes he would come home from a trip unannounced.

?!

SURPRISE!!!

DADDY!!

He even arranged for others to surprise us.

So Rin... I hope you don't mind, I invited my cousin to our sleepover.

Oh? Uh, okay... I guess...

That's kinda awkward since I never actually *met* Claud's cousin.

And here she is!

Boo! heh heh heh...

!

MANETTE!!!

I thought you said your *cousin* was sleeping over!

She's *my* cousin too, remember?

"The 3 Musketeers"

How long has Dad been gone?

Five weeks, his longest trip ever. I can't wait to see him tomorrow.

Oops... pardon me...

BUMP

AY! AY! TONY! YOU'RE BACK!

...oh, and Daniel and I got tickets to "Me and My Girl" for tomorrow...

Tintin in Tibet

?

Tintin in Tibet

DADDY!!!

Surprise! heh heh...

Surprise, Princess!! HAH! Got you!

DADDY!! I *knew* it! Ha ha ha!

SURPRISE!

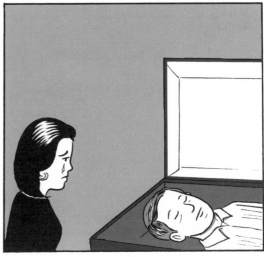

My cousin Ico and his wife, Janine, arrive. They have just flown in from Dumaguete.

My dad was the favorite uncle of most of my cousins, but he had lived with Ico's family when he was younger, and later on they worked together managing the clan's farms. He was like a father to Ico.

When Ico sees the coffin, he is devastated, sobbing and calling out loud to my dad.

I have always felt a certain kinship towards Ico, which began when I was nine years old.

At the time, to be nearer to my school, I spent much of my 4th and 5th grades sleeping at my lola's house, where Ico and his family also lived.

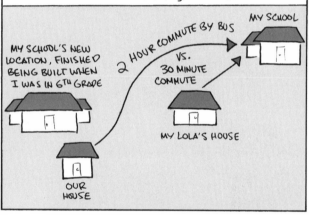

MY SCHOOL

MY SCHOOL'S NEW LOCATION, FINISHED BEING BUILT WHEN I WAS IN 6TH GRADE

2 HOUR COMMUTE BY BUS

VS.

30 MINUTE COMMUTE

MY LOLA'S HOUSE

OUR HOUSE

Lola Loring would permit me to watch only one TV show, "Little House on the Prairie". (The rest were too immoral.) As fascinating as it was to see Michael Landon bursting into tears every Sunday night (which I don't recall Pa Ingalls doing in any of the books), it wasn't enough to fill those long hours when I was away from my family.

Caroline...

Charles!

Ico's family were all grown-ups, either working or at university, so I had no one to play with. Ico was ten years older than me but he must've taken pity on my boredom because he taught me how to shoot hoops in their driveway.

He was very patient and after a while I really got the hang of it.

When he wasn't there, I practiced for hours. I loved sports and liked seeing how good I was getting.

I enjoyed the repetition of it. I'd practice till it was dark and the mosquitoes started eating me alive.

A few months later, the boy cousins decided to play a game of 21. Naturally, I wanted to join.

No way! No girls allowed! You don't even know how to shoot!

Yes I do! Why can't I join? I'll tell Daddy!

And...

Of course she can play!

Hah! See?

But she doesn't even know how!

Two points!

25

I ended up beating all the boys and winning easily!

Why Princess! You're full of surprises!

Manong Ico taught me.

Some years later, just before my wedding, my dad took me to the farms in Negros.* Ico was there and just as nice and brotherly as ever.

Wow you're all grown up!

*pronounced "Neg-raws"

Negros is where my dad's family of sugar planters hails from. We visited the ancestral home which was built in the late 1800s and today is a museum.

Although known for its grand staircases and eighteen rooms, the thing I liked most was that my great-great grandmother's bedroom had a secret passage and peepholes to spy on servants!

We also visited their house in Fortuna, where my dad spent his summers.

Tito Minggoy and I used to sleep in that room. One night we locked the door so we wouldn't have to share our candy...

He told me anecdotes from his childhood (all of which I'd heard before!).

And the next morning when we woke up we were surrounded by slippers! HA HA HA!

26

He introduced me to the farm hands who were harvesting sugar cane.

My daughter Rina.

He showed me their latest venture: prawn-farming.

Every night at the hacienda there was fresh prawn tempura, as much as I could eat.

Thank you.

In a few days I would be married and moving to Canada.

Look Princess... whenever I see a full moon I think of you. You always loved full moons so much, no?

When I look back on that visit, I think playing tour guide was my dad's way of making sure I would always remember where I came from.

Just look at that view, Princess! Wow!

By then, Ico had his own family and lived in another area of the farms.

My wife, Jeanine.

Hi!

I think that after my mom, my siblings and me, it's Ico who feels the loss of my dad the most.

How tragic that three sons of Loring died violently. Isyong -- plane crash. Obet -- murdered. And now Tony.

It's like the Kennedys, no?

It's a blessing *prima**Loring isn't around anymore. I think it would have been too much for her.

Yes. Tony was always Mama's favourite.

*cousin

28

My dad's mother Loreto, whom we all called Lola Loring, was a deeply religious and devout Roman Catholic who would hear mass seven days a week.

She was the proud matriarch of eight children and forty grandchildren.

Beneath her kindly grandmotherly exterior lay a forceful personality and fierce temper that unleashed itself when her demands weren't met. My cousin Iyoy slyly called her "Der Fuhrer" behind her back because when she got angry, everyone was afraid.

Scene from the 2004 film "The Downfall" where Hitler, upon hearing the allied forces have triumphed, gives his officers hell.

Lola Loring when she lost her temper.

Not even the brashest, most smart-alec cousins were bold enough to face her wrath.

Gerry, turn off the TV so we can pray the rosary.

But Lola! It's the last quarter of the finals!

Pardon me...?

The First Sorrowful Mystery is...

When I stayed at her house, I slept in her room, on my dead grandpa's bed. The mattress was hard as a rock and even if it was stifling, to save electricity, we rarely used air-conditioning.

ow....

My dad's great-grandparents were wealthy landowners who made their fortunes in sugarcane farming during the 19ᵀᴴ century.

Their descendants branched out into various industries, attended university abroad and were prominent in business and politics.

My grandfather, Placido Lizares Mapa, was Secretary of Agriculture and a co-founder of Metrobank, today the largest bank in the Philippines. My grandmother Loreto Ledesma was an heiress to a shipping company.

My *lola* told me that before the war, she'd been different, very materialistic. She travelled in style and bought the most expensive fashions and jewelry.

But along came World War II and the Japanese occupation. With each new threat to her family, Loreto made promises to God that she would devote her life to religion if He protected them from harm. As she grew more devout, her perspective on life was forever changed.

In the years after the war, and especially after my grandfather's death in 1967, *lola* Loring saw no importance in increasing her fortune, giving most of it away to various religious groups and charities. To her children's dismay, she divided her inheritance among her siblings (none of whom, it must be said, possessed the same moral qualms about increasing *their* wealth).

Her favorite biblical verses were all the ones to do with being poor. She was famous for her austerity.

"For the love of money is the root of all evil." Timothy 6:4/11

"No one can serve two masters. Either he will hate the one and love the other, or he will be devoted to the one and despise the other. You cannot serve both God and Money." Matthew 6:24

"Blessed are you who are poor, for yours is the kingdom of heaven." Luke 6:20-21

"It is easier for a camel to go through the eye of a needle than for a rich man to enter the kingdom of God." Mark 10:25

"Then Jesus beholding him loved him, and said unto him, One thing thou lackest: go thy way, sell whatsoever thou hast, and give to the poor, and thou shalt have treasure in heaven: and come, take up the cross, and follow me." Mark 10:21

Although she could easily afford a Mercedes, for years she rode around in a station wagon so old we called it "Methuselah".

When she heard mass at her local church in Forbes Park, Methuselah stood out like a sore thumb amongst the various luxury cars.

She had an antique piano that was never tuned, but it was probably for the best. Mothers didn't need to worry that their kids were breaking it.

Because I slept there so often, *lola* taught me the art of taking a bath using just half a pail of water.

① Pour one *tabo** of water to wet your head and body.

② Shampoo your hair.

* pail

31

③ Thoroughly wet a facecloth and rub soap into it till it's sudsy.

④ Scrub your body all over.

⑤ Wring out facecloth, then wet it again and wash your body.

⑥ Using the *tabo*, rinse all the shampoo and soap from your hair and body with the remaining water in the pail.

Total water consumption: 4 liters

Total water consumption of an average five minute shower: 40 liters

How to wash your hands using just one small bowl of water:

① In the sink, start with a plastic bowl already filled with water.

② Dip your hands in the water, then lather up using a bar of soap.

③ Scrub your hands thoroughly with the soap suds.

④ Pour the dirty, sudsy water into the sink.

⑤ To finish, turn on the faucet and run fresh water into the bowl while holding your already clean hands underneath for a final rinse.

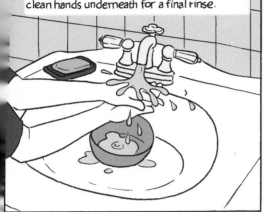

You now have clean water in the bowl, ready for the next use!

My *lola*'s obsession with water conservation meant her indoor pool remained unused, dry as a bone. She said her water bill was already too high to maintain it.

One day, during typhoon season, it rained so hard that water gushed through the open skylight into the pool. Someone had plugged the drainhole and pretty soon, the pool started to fill up.

Tonton had the idea to try and fill the rest of the pool using just rainwater. So a bunch of energetic cousins grabbed buckets and formed a human chain, collecting the water that was coming down in floods and torrents through the drainpipes outside.

We actually got it halfway filled!

WHEEE!

On the way home, I overheard my mom drily say to my dad:

Why doesn't Mama just fill up the pool? Then the kids wouldn't have to wait for a typhoon to go swimming!

My dad wouldn't hear of one bad word said against his mother.

Yes, but look at how much fun they had!

Yeah, right!

Loreto had five married sons. Their wives (who jokingly called themselves the "outlaws") formed a common bond in realizing two things: ① Attendance at *lola's* scheduled family gatherings was mandatory, and ② their side always came second.

THE ~~IN-LAWS~~ *Outlaws*

| CHONA | GENE | LIRIO | MARILYN | LULAY |

Of all her children, my dad was the most devoted to Loreto. He could never say no to her and always at the expense, it seemed, of my long-suffering mom.

Of course we'll be there, Mama.

Tony, it's Noel's opening night, remember?

We might have to leave early, but for sure we'll be there.

Tony, can we not for once skip dinner at Forbes? This is a big production and Noel is the lead!

Noel's show starts at eight. We have plenty of time to do both.

My mom's brother, Noel, and his wife Lally, arrive at the wake. They are very close to my parents.

Hello, *hija.**

For once, *tito* Noel had no jokes.

Noel, a famous actor, was best known as one half of a comedic duo with his portly partner Subas Herrero. They were the "Laurel and Hardy" of the Philippines", and in the 1980s had starred in a hit variety show with the wonderfully random name "Champoy".

He was married to Lally Laurel, a granddaughter of former Philippine president Jose P. Laurel. (She herself was a congresswoman.) They had three children -- Trixie, Joel and Michael. Their family was outgoing, the life of the party, hammy in the best possible way, and lovers of Broadway musicals.

HA CHA!

* actual photo

Our Sunday routine was to all have lunch at my maternal grandfather's house. *Lolo* Koko's wife, Lina, died in 1976, and it showed. My mom would often comment on the state of the house she'd grown up in.

TSK! So dirty! I'm sure Lola Lina is rolling in her grave!

I wish you could've seen how nice this place was in its heyday.*

* My mom loves to use well-worn phrases like "rolling in her grave" and "heyday".

Manang Basyon may not have been a good housekeeper, but she was an excellent cook.

NILAGA, a clear soup made with chunks of beef, potatoes, bok choy and bone marrow

LUMPIA Spring rolls filled with meat and vegetables, deep-fried and served with a sweet and sour sauce

CROQUETTAS Ground pork and potato patties fried in oil

ADOBO, chicken marinated in soy sauce, vinegar, garlic and peppercorns, sautéed and then fried

HALABOS NA HIPON Fresh shrimp cooked in its shell

*dear

We had the exact same dishes every Sunday. Our stomachs and taste buds, Pavlovian-like, would set their juices churning and salivating in anticipation.

AAAAHH

After lunch the men would play poker while the women went shopping. We kids would set off to the neighbourhood *tindahan** to buy candy.

* *tindahan* : store

We'd get back in time for the *taho* guy. *Taho* is one of my favourite things to eat, ever. It's made up of white, silky smooth bean curd, brown sugar sauce and *sago* (tapioca) balls. It may not sound appetizing but it's the best!

TAHO-O-O TAHO-O-O

Every week, those gluttons Joel and Michael fought over who would get to use the biggest bowl in the kitchen.

HAH! Shrimp!

GRRR!

The *taho* guy would scoop the smooth white bean curd into our bowls with his flat ladle, gently drizzle that with syrup, and finally top it all off with *sago** balls. We would watch, mesmerized, as he prepared every bowl with the attention of a sous-chef at a five-star restaurant.

OOOH

AHHH

*tapioca

Once in a while, the men would play golf instead of poker, and we kids got to spend the afternoon at Noelally's house. Those were our Sundays, and one day in 1984...

Buster! You're so fat!

Hey cuz, come and listen to this...

I was fourteen and heavily into Depeche Mode. Joel made me sit in his dad's sound-proof recording studio in total darkness (for maximum effect) to listen to their latest single.

♪ I DON'T WANT TO START ANY BLASPHEMOUS RUMOURS BUT I THINK THAT GOD'S GOT A SICK SENSE OF HUMOUR ♪

Whoa...

I know, right?

AND WHEN I DIE ♪ I EXPECT TO FIND HIM LAAAUUUGHING

B-BUMP

B-BUMP

I felt very strange listening to those lyrics.

? ? ? ? ?

Religion in the Philippines has a powerful, almost overwhelming presence. It is a country that is 85% Roman Catholic, and every weekend churches are filled with worshippers.

We are, after all, the country famous for staging crucifixions every Easter, to the fascination of the rest of the world.

Children memorize a litany of prayers at an early age and have religious studies in school.

What are the 9 Choirs of Angels?

Seraphim, Cherubim, Thrones, Dominations Virtues, Powers, Principalities, Archangels.

Oh! And Angels.

Every household has a picture of the Sacred Heart. (It's practically the law)

Given these levels of devotion in our country, one would assume we are made up of scary religious fundamentalists like those found in the Bible Belt or the Middle East.

JAY-ZUS!

However, this isn't the case, and I have some theories (completely unscientific, unproven and unresearched) as to why.

WHY RELIGION HASN'T TURNED FILIPINOS INTO ANGRY, SCARY FUNDAMENTALISTS

THEORY #1

THE VIRGIN MARY IS HUGE IN THE PHILIPPINES

Her image is found simply everywhere. She is either smiling benevolently or looking sorrowful about something you've done.

There is this underlying feeling that no matter how much you screw up, the Virgin Mary, mother of all mothers, will forgive you. And since she *is* the mother of Jesus, God will forgive you too. And if God and Mary can forgive anyone, who are we to judge someone else and say they'll burn in hell?

Maybe this is why *lola* Loring, for all her staunch, conservative Catholicism, employed two men whom we all knew as "Edna" (the cook) and "Frieda" (the house boy). No one seemed to think this was the least bit strange.

EDNA

Ay! I broke a nail!

FRIEDA

Another positive outcome of having the Virgin Mary as such an important figure is that women by association are elevated to a status of equality and even reverence not often seen in the rest of the world, establishing the Philippines as a matriarchial society.

OTHER COUNTRIES

PHILIPPINES

Catholicism was first introduced to the Philippines by Spanish conquerors and missionaries in the 16th century.

I like to think that way back then, the native women realized they could have a good thing going if they made the Virgin Mary the country's most important religious icon.

And this is Mary, the Mother of God.

Hmmm...

This way, Filipino men would be indoctrinated from the start that *all* women, just like the mother of Jesus, were to be loved and cherished.

(And if the country ever had to be led by a woman, it would be natural and not something to fear or scoff at. But more on that later.)

This might be why the men who consider themselves very macho and are out all night drinking with the guys while joking that a woman's place is in the kitchen are the same ones who hand their paychecks over to their wives and can't say no to their mothers.

We're visiting my mother later.

Yes dear.

It's strange how personal whims can result in entire countries going through lasting change. King Henry VIII ended England's ties with the Catholic Church because they wouldn't let him divorce his wife to marry another.

Well then we'll be Anglican! So there!

Then there's the myth of a king in Spain who was born with a speech impediment which made him unable to pronounce the "ss" sound. All his life, he spoke with a lisp.

Grathiath.

Buenoth Diath.

His court followed suit.

Grathiath.

Buenoth Diath.

To this day in areas of Spain, people use the "th" sound for "s". It's a myth denounced by scholars and historians, but who can really say for sure?

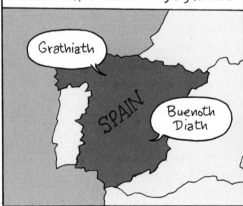

Grathiath

SPAIN

Buenoth Diath

Did something comparable happen in certain countries that would explain the misogyny that exists there? Why else would some cultures treat women the way they do?

WHY???

I don't get it.

40

Maybe thousands of years ago, certain would-be rulers had mothers who were cruel to them as children and as a result decreed a hatred for all women which was passed down through the centuries.

No .... m-mamau...

I see no other way of explaining the kind of culture where men think it's normal and even desirable to mistreat women, a culture which has developed in so many countries ...

Beat her, rape her, torture her... I don't care.

You heard his Majesty, boys! Woo hoo!

Innocent girl →

WHY RELIGION HASN'T TURNED FILIPINOS INTO ANGRY, SCARY FUNDAMENTALISTS

THEORY # 2

RELIGION IS BASED ON GUILT, NOT FEAR

Religious fundamentalist views based on fear -- fear that God will punish you for your sins, that you will burn in eternal hell, that heathens will take over the world -- create conditions of fearfulness towards anyone who thinks differently from you. But guilt is different. There is no anger, hate or violence. Guilt is when you feel you've let down someone you love.

Fear leads to anger, anger leads to hate...

Yoda

Guilt is God's way of letting you know you're having too good a time.

Dennis Miller

Luckily there is a solution for all that guilt: The Sacrament of Confession.

Spent the night with a mistress? No problem! Just confess your sins the next morning and you can receive Communion again.

The body of Christ...

Amen.

Whew!

Imagine Organized Religion as a very strict, heavy-handed, authoritarian father. Each of his children, depending on personality, temperament and place in the family will have a different relationship with him throughout their lives.

The oldest usually feels the burden of responsibility. He is a dutiful son, but his feelings towards his father are a mix of love and awe and fear, always the fear that his father will only love him so long as he obeys. And he does obey. He fervently honors his father. But he is righteous and angry with the rest of the world.

The Fervent Worshipper

Then there is the child who, while growing up, is desperate to please. He's been indoctrinated into obeying all the rules. Even when he is an adult, he never feels the need to question authority. Being told what to do makes him feel safe.

The **Unquestioning Fundamentalist**

Another type of child feels oppressed by such authority. He causes the most trouble growing up and is in constant conflict, openly rebelling against all rules. Eventually his relationship with his father breaks down. He leaves the family and finds his own path in life.

The Non-Believer

Organized Religion

Another child does find many of the rules questionable but follows most of them to keep the peace. He respects his father without necessarily agreeing with him. Later on he is busy with his own life but still tries to visit when he can.

The Average Church-Goer

The baby of the family is happy-go-lucky, social, breaks the rules (often!) but since he can charm his father, he keeps on having his cake and eating it too, secure in the knowledge that he is unconditionally loved.

The Fun-Loving Follower

This is the Filipino, and unlike his siblings, his relationship with his father is uncomplicated, affectionate and loving. And so...

WHY RELIGION HASN'T TURNED FILIPINOS INTO ANGRY, SCARY FUNDAMENTALISTS

THEORY # 3

FILIPINOS JUST WANNA HAVE FUN

(WITH APOLOGIES TO CINDI LAUPER)

Filipinos are the most social, fun-loving people in the world. A lonely Filipino is a rare creature indeed. We are constantly surrounded by family, friends, friends of family, and family of friends. Whether we like it or not.

Tito Nonoy · Manang Iyay · Marites · Nini · Manong Ino · Father Chito · Mammy · Sister Loretto · Javi · Paco · Mari · Nina · Chinie · Leah · Deanna · Manette · Tito Ferdi · Ninang Renee · Nick

There is always a party to go to, a dinner to attend, someone's birthday / wedding / baptism / confirmation / shower / anniversary / etc. etc. etc. All that socializing means people don't actually have the chance to simmer with self-righteous anger.

Anton · Chino · Suzette · Bimsy · Bernice · Misel

Look at those homosexual infidels! An abomination to God!

Let us stone them!

OTHER COUNTRIES

Look at those *baklas**! So unnatural!

Let's... hey, is that karaoke?

PHILIPPINES

I suspect Filipinos are simply too busy partying to condemn anyone who is different to burn in hell.

LET ME IN WITH THE FLOWERS DON'T BRING ME DOWN I'M ON THE GROUND ♪

LAST NIGHT I HURT YOU SO BUT TILL THE MORNIN' SUN GROWS COLD AND RIVERS FLOW ♂

Anyway, to this day when I hear "Blasphemous Rumours", I'm taken back to the shock and strange thrill I felt when I realized for the first time that not everyone in the world believed in God, much less a benevolent one.

B-BUMP   B-BUMP

B-BUMP

* gays

43

This loss of innocence was an unsettling shift in my world view, which so far had been influenced by my culture, my family, and certainly my school...

It was an all-girls private Catholic school where I went from the ages of 8-16, and a particularly religious one even by Philippine standards.

There was daily mass in the chapel every morning, attended mostly by parents and teachers.

One year we had a new and very young priest named Father Santos. He looked like an even cuter version of Jon Moss, the drummer of the Culture Club.

Morning mass attendance among high school students increased dramatically.

Father Santos always looked so nervous (and, we agreed, so sweet and adorable) during the entire mass.

He reminded me of a deep-sea diver in his protective cage, surrounded by longing, hungry sharks.

One day, a beautiful fourth year student went and confessed her sins to him...

Bless me Father, for I have sinned... I am having strong feelings for someone... and that someone is... *you*, Father.

The next week, we had a new priest saying mass. Lookswise, he was more of the Mr. Bean variety.

We never heard from Father Santos again.

My school curriculum included Latin, Philosophy and Theology. In music class we studied Debussy and Rimski Korsakov. For English Literature, we read Chaucer, Homer, Sophocles and Longfellow. All in all, a seemingly well-rounded education, Right?

Well, unfortunately, the group of religious people who founded my school did *NOT* believe in girls playing sports. Possibly they feared sports would encourage ≥GASP≤ lesbian tendencies.

This was during the 1980s, not the 1950s!

Thus for our P.E. uniform, we wore bloomers instead of shorts.

Gym class consisted of calisthenics, a little volleyball, and learning to dance to the Glenn Miller Band.

♪ IN THE MOOD··· ♪

How I longed to play real sports like soccer or basketball!

What the teachers failed to understand is that we all have masculine and feminine traits which have nothing to do with sexual orientation but which nevertheless need to be expressed.

Yaya, can you please wash my P.E. uniform? I have a game tomorrow.

Not fair...

The part of me that wanted to express myself through sports but wasn't allowed, rebelled and found another way. I simply became as tomboyish as possible.

At games with my cousins, I insisted on being "skins" for as long as my chest would permit.

45

I kept refusing to wear dresses unless my mom threatened me. But once in a while, an aunt would say:

Why do you dress that way? Are you a boy or a girl?

Well, why not? She's comfortable!

Come, Rin.

My mom's mother, Carolina Flores, was born in 1914. She was an accomplished woman who was ahead of her time.

She was an award-winning journalist who created the popular soap opera "Gulong Ng Palad" under the pen name Lina Flor.

Lina Flor

- The Manila Times
- The Daily Mirror
- Kislap Graphic
- Liwayway
- Herald Magazine

Lina was a very petite 4'10 in heels, with a doll-like figure and fine, high cheekbones. She was quite beautiful and graceful.

With my grandfather, Francisco "Koko" Trinidad

My grandfather Francisco Trinidad was a broadcaster known as the "Father of Philippine Radio". As journalists, he and Lina socialized with politicians, movie stars and all manner of high society.

With President and First Lady Magsaysay at Malacañang Palace

With stars from Sampaguita Studios movie productions

With the Queen of Thailand during a state visit

When my mom was born, she was the fourth child, a girl after three boys, and much anticipated as the first and only daughter of Lina Flor.

Whereas my mom took after her father's looks, her brother Noel, one year older, had Lina's fine features.

Noel inherited what Spanish blood was running in the family and was what Filipinos refer to as "mestizo". He was much admired and petted by the visiting socialites.

Well hello there, handsome.

As my mom remembers it, the visiting socialites were not so admiring of her.

What a plain little girl. Especially for the daughter of Lina, no?

What a pity about her nose.

And her brother so guapo* too.

* handsome

47

When I look at my mom's teenage pictures, modelling for my dad, very waif-like a la Audrey Hepburn, it's hard to believe she actually felt plain, even ugly.

She has always been beautiful, graceful and ladylike.

Especially next to my sisters and me!

My mom often spoke of the constant pressure she felt growing up as Lina Flor's daughter, being judged for her looks and found wanting.

I think her experiences made her unusually tolerant of my tomboyish ways. Still, I'm sure she wondered why I apparently had inherited nothing of my Lola Lina.

⸘SIGH⸘

Look Mommy! I can head the ball!

But as soon as any hint arose of some *tita* clucking in disapproval, my mom was the first to protect me.

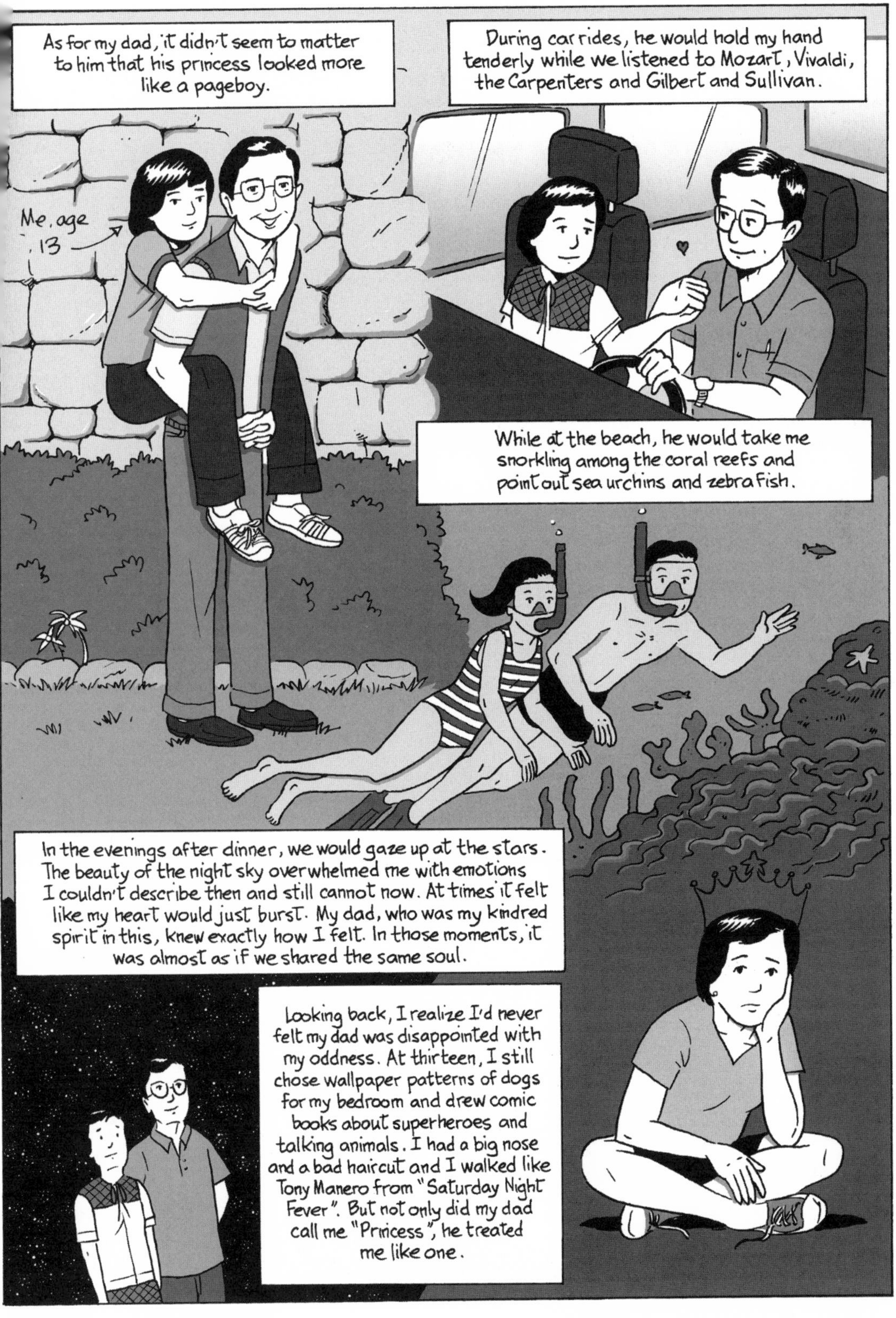

As for my dad, it didn't seem to matter to him that his princess looked more like a pageboy.
During car rides, he would hold my hand tenderly while we listened to Mozart, Vivaldi, the Carpenters and Gilbert and Sullivan.
Me, age 13
While at the beach, he would take me snorkling among the coral reefs and point out sea urchins and zebra fish.
In the evenings after dinner, we would gaze up at the stars. The beauty of the night sky overwhelmed me with emotions I couldn't describe then and still cannot now. At times it felt like my heart would just burst. My dad, who was my kindred spirit in this, knew exactly how I felt. In those moments, it was almost as if we shared the same soul.
Looking back, I realize I'd never felt my dad was disappointed with my oddness. At thirteen, I still chose wallpaper patterns of dogs for my bedroom and drew comic books about superheroes and talking animals. I had a big nose and a bad haircut and I walked like Tony Manero from "Saturday Night Fever". But not only did my dad call me "Princess", he treated me like one.

One day on August 21, 1983, we were at the Trinidads' house to celebrate tito Noel's birthday. The grown-ups then left for Manila airport to join a party of people who were welcoming Senator Aquino back to the Philippines.

WELCOME HOME NINOY!

My parents weren't coming back till late afternoon which was fine by me. I could finally read my cousin Trixie's massive collection of Richie Rich comic books.

← All Richie Rich!

Richie Rich

Four hours and forty comic books later, the grown-ups returned.

SLAM

I CANNOT BELIEVE IT!!

?

Richie Rich

They were extremely upset.

What's the matter?

Yeah, what's going on?

HE WAS SHOT!! NINOY IS DEAD!!!

That bastard Marcos! Of course he's behind this.

Senator Benigno Aquino Jr. (affectionately known as "Ninoy") was a leader of the opposition against the current president, Ferdinand Marcos.

Ninoy

Marcos

Marcos was first elected President in 1965. His autocratic style of leadership brought violent public protests and in 1972 he responded by declaring Martial Law. Thus the Philippines went from a democracy to a dictatorship.

With the military completely under his control, Marcos awarded government positions to his and his wife Imelda's relatives and jailed his political opponents, most notably Ninoy Aquino.

In 1980, after eight years in prison, Aquino suffered a series of heart attacks. He was allowed to have surgery in the U.S. if he agreed to relocate there with his entire family and remain in exile.

Meanwhile, during almost two decades in office, Marcos and Imelda steadily amassed a huge fortune by embezzling billions of dollars from the country's coffers. In the face of rampant poverty, they bought multi-million dollar properties around the world, built lavish mansions and lived like royalty.

Yet for all their dizzying wealth, the Marcoses were incredibly tacky. There was a pathetic neediness in the nouveau-riche ways they tried to impress their high society counterparts around the world. Like a woman possessed, Imelda would go on million-dollar shopping sprees, collecting priceless jewelry and artwork the way other people collect comic books and baseball cards.

Imelda's pursuit of decadence was astounding. She was a modern-day Marie-Antoinette, openly flaunting her extravagant lifestyle, and scornful of the millions of Filipinos who lived in extreme poverty.

I have to look beautiful so that the poor Filipinos will have a star to look at from their slums. *

* Yes, she actually said that

Sometimes Imelda's schemes would backfire in a very public way. She built the ostentatious Coconut Palace for Pope John Paul II to stay in during his visit in 1981. But appalled that it cost 40 million pesos in a country filled with such poverty, the Pope declined her invitation.

Er... no Thanks.

Imelda dreamed of a film festival to rival Cannes. She commissioned the Manila Film Center and modeled it after the Parthenon. It cost 25 million dollars and was to be completed in time for the 1981 Manila International Film Fest.

As the deadline loomed, a crew of 4,000 working around the clock tried to finish in time. But then a scaffolding collapsed, sending over a hundred workers tumbling into the wet cement below.

AHHH!

CRACK

The story goes that since it would've taken too much time to retrieve the bodies, Imelda ordered construction to go on as scheduled. The fallen workers were covered with cement, thus buried alive.

GLOOP

The festival opened on schedule and international stars unknowingly celebrated on top of what had become a tomb!

Ever since then, ghosts have been sighted roaming the building. It's said the Manila Film Center is one of the most haunted places in the Philippines.

Believe It or Not!

Whether a factual account or an urban legend, the important thing is how readily Filipinos believe this story to be true. Such is the reputation of Imelda.

...and they were BURIED ALIVE!

That is one cold bitch.

When it came to delusions of grandeur, Marcos was no slouch himself, ordering a massive Mt. Rushmore-like concrete bust in his own image built on a cliff overlooking the South China Sea.

Many Filipinos, once loyal to their country and hopeful for better days, grew jaded and yearned to leave. My parents were among those looking to migrate to North America.

For a country so rich in natural resources and which once showed such promise, the Philippines was dying a slow death caused by government corruption and the excesses of Marcos's regime.

Ninoy Aquino, living comfortably with his family in Boston, was aggrieved by this state of affairs and decided enough was enough.

I have to suffer with my people.

53

Despite warnings from the military, Aquino insisted on returning to the Philippines. When asked about the death threats issued by pro-Marcos groups, Ninoy said:

The Filipino is worth dying for.

They were prophetic words. As soon as he got off the plane, a military escort appeared and whisked him out through a side door. Seconds later, shots rang out. Then Aquino lay dead on the tarmac. He never did touch his native soil.

Beside Aquino, also dead, was his supposed assassin. The military escort immediately dumped both bodies in an awaiting vehicle and left. The whole thing was captured on film by a Japanese television crew.

AVSECOM

The Marcos government would later claim that the second body was the lone gunman responsible for Aquino's death.

The entire country knew otherwise.

A sleeping giant, previously apathetic to the injustices committed over the past two decades, had been awakened from its stupor by the brutal martyrdom of a beloved son coming home. The funeral procession, an eleven-hour, 30 kilometer march through Metro Manila, was attended by millions. It was more than a funeral -- it was a political demonstration.

Filipinos are a peaceful, gentle people, to the point where U.S. politicians had sneered at the country's meekness over the years in submitting to the Marcos regime's excesses.

But this latest incident was too much. Filipinos' sense of morality was outraged to the core, and the response was electrifying. Over the next 24 months, the nation erupted in protest after protest.

Historically, political demonstrations have been the arena of the student, the radical, the oppressed lower class. Crucially, this time was different.

OUR RIGHT

JUSTICE FOR JUSTICE FOR ALL OPPRESSION!

VISION OF OUR RIGHT!

JUSTICE FOR ALL

MACKAISA ITIGIL ANG PANUPIL SA MGA ANG KARAPATAN

KATARUNON KAY NINOY AT SA LAHAT NG BIKTIMA NG PAMPULITIKANG KARAHASAN!

KATA MO Y

LAHA

FIGHT POLITICAL OPPRESSION!

GLE

MACLING DULAG   DR BOBBY DE LA CRUZ   EDGAR JOPSON   DR. JOHNNY ESCANDAR   NINOY AQUINO

JUSTICE FOR NINOY/JUSTICE FOR ALL VICTIMS OF POLITICAL REPRESSION AND MILITARY TERRORISM!!

NINOY NINOY

Now, business executives and wealthy socialites were marching alongside jeepney drivers, sales clerks and street vendors. Bank presidents, secretaries, doctors, lawyers, priests, nuns, housewives, grandmothers and grade schoolers -- all plunged into the fray.

The country's political drama spilled into 1984, the year I cut my hair like Simon Le Bon of Duran Duran (my latest obsession).

SIGH

I was fourteen, and apart from my school uniform, I only wore jeans, polo shirts and sneakers. My mom later told me she prayed a lot of novenas as she worried I'd end up never marrying (apparently the worst fate a Filipino mother could imagine for her daughter).

Please God, let her become a *real* girl!!

But she was comforted by the fact that over the years, I harboured crush after crush on a litany of actors and pop stars. It turns out that despite my tomboyish ways on the outside, I was actually totally boy crazy on the inside.

Bob from Sesame Street, age 5

Mel Gibson age 13

Harrison Ford, age 11

The Six Million Dollar Man, age 7

Shaun Cassidy, age 9

Duran Duran age 14

I had the biggest crush on Christopher Reeve. The "Superman" movies and "Somewhere in Time" were on a constant loop in our house.

I heard Chris was in a movie called "Deathtrap" where he and Michael Caine play gay lovers and actually kiss (a big deal in those days).

56

Worried that my conservative parents wouldn't let me watch it, I snuck a viewing at my cousin Deanna's house.

Why is that old guy kissing Superman?

Shut up, Javi.

I watched "Ladyhawke" in theatres and for months afterwards fantasized about Rutger Hauer.

Navarre! ♥

When we rented Betamax tapes, we were able to keep them for a week. This allowed for repeated viewings and I soon became obsessed with scenes from two movies: Patrick Swayze in "Uncommon Valour"...

Y-y-you... y-you... c-can't keep me... from... THIS MISSION!

...and Richard Gere in "An Officer and A Gentleman".

I got nowhere else to go!

Both scenes had the actors bursting into tears in a way that broke my heart.

I rewound and watched endlessly, mesmerized by Richard Gere's blinking.

I got nowhere else to go!

One day I was in my *lolo's* attic, hunting for something to read, when I found an old paperback biography of the actor James Dean, whom I'd never heard of before.

?

James Dean

It was written in the 1950s, totally unauthorized, and used a cheesy, melodramatic style of the time. According to the author, "Jimmy" Dean was lonely and misunderstood, his life full of suffering and angst, and like a little boy, his only desire was to be loved.

Naturally, I was hooked.

I watched "Rebel Without A Cause", "East of Eden" and "Giant" in quick succession.

You're tearing me apart!!!

Then, because there were no more films to see, I read John Steinbeck's "East of Eden" just so I could imagine Dean as the troubled Cal Trask.

This obsession to learn all I could about actors I had crushes on during those teenage years has served me well. As one role led to another, I grew to love old movies and I ended up absorbing all kinds of culture I wouldn't have known of otherwise.

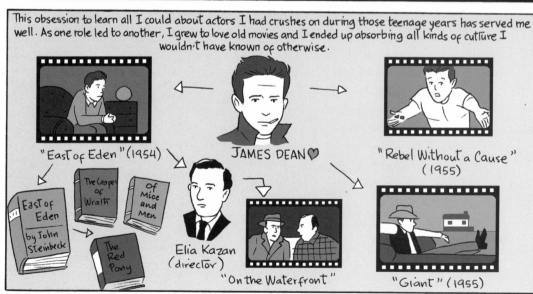

"East of Eden" (1954)

East of Eden by John Steinbeck

The Grapes of Wrath

Of Mice and Men

The Red Pony

JAMES DEAN ♡

Elia Kazan (director)

"On the Waterfront"

"Rebel Without a Cause" (1955)

"Giant" (1955)

♡ GREGORY PECK

"The Keys of The Kingdom" (1944) by AJ Cronin

"To Kill A Mockingbird" by Harper Lee (1962)

"Snows of Kilimanjaro" (1952) by Ernest Hemmingway

The Art of Saluadore Dali

"Spellbound" (1945)

"Rebecca" (1940)

Alfred Hitchcock

"To Catch a Thief" (1955)

CARY GRANT

Judy Judy Judy

"Notorious" (1946)

"The Birds" (1963)

"Vertigo" (1958)

"North by Northwest" (1959)

"His Girl Friday" (1940)

ROD TAYLOR

"The Time Machine" by H.G. Wells (1960)

THE TIME MACHINE

"Psycho" (1960)

The scores of Bernard Herrmann

♥ MONTGOMERY CLIFT

"A Place in The Sun" (1951)

"An American Tragedy" THEODORE DREISER

"An American Tragedy" by Theodore Dreiser

Marlon Brando

"A Streetcar Named Desire" (1951) by Tennessee Williams

"The Heiress" (1949)

"From Here to Eternity" (1953)

GENE KELLY ♥

"Singin' in the Rain" (1952)

"An American in Paris" (1951)

MUSICALS!

"West Side Story" (1961)

"My Fair Lady" (1964)

"Oliver!" (1968)

PYGMALION

"Pygmalion" by George Bernard Shaw

MY FAIR LADY

"My Fair Lady" by Alan Jay Lerner

♥ REX HARRISON
(yes, strangely I did have a crush on him)

"Doctor Dolittle" (1967)

Doctor Dolittle

by Hugh Lofting

and finally...

The Cast of "The Outsiders"

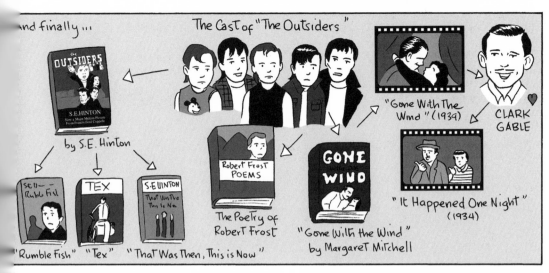

by S.E. Hinton

"Rumble Fish" "Tex" "That Was Then, This is Now"

The Poetry of Robert Frost

"Gone With the Wind" by Margaret Mitchell

"Gone With The Wind" (1939)

CLARK GABLE

"It Happened One Night" (1934)

When I first read "The Outsiders", my fourteen year old's sensibilities were blown away by S.E. Hinton's cleverness in ending the book by looping it with the beginning.

WHEN I STEPPED OUT into the bright sunlight from the darkness of the movie house, I had only two things on my mind: Paul Newman and a ride home. I was wishing I looked

Ponyboy's assignment for English was to write a theme ("as long as you want") and "The Outsiders" was that theme. It was a reason for the book to exist, which made it even more real to me.

But that is SO COOL!

So this book isn't just Ponyboy's story... it's also how and why he wrote his story to begin with!

Isn't that great??

Okay already!

My numerous crushes were not limited to actors by any means. I fancied Sting something fierce. It all started when I saw him remove his shirt in a music video.

GULP!

PLEASE DON'T STAND SO CLOSE TO MEEEEEE

61

I listened to "Synchronicity II" every day after school, drumming my way through the entire album using chopsticks, pillows and tupperware.

I bought a paperback set of Mervyn Peake's "The Gormenghast Trilogy" because Sting said they were his favourite books. (I never made it past chapter 2.)

My favourite Police song was "King of Pain", which opens with descending piano notes full of pathos. When they reached a particular chord, my heart felt like it was being squeezed.

Everything about that song spoke to me, the lyrical angst, the melancholy. I played it and felt no one understood the depths of my sadness.

Except Sting... he understands!

IS MY SOUL UP THERE...

Tears for Fears' album "The Hurting" was all about suffering. I hadn't yet discovered The Smiths (one of the great loves of my life) but "The Hurting" was definitely a precursor.

There is a certain window in age (for me it was between 11 and 18) when your reaction to music is so powerful and pure that nothing you listen to afterwards can grab at your emotions in the same way.

I love Pearl Jam, Nirvana, the Chili Peppers, GNR... but even these bands came at the tail end of that almost unbearably nostalgic age. Their music can't stop me in my tracks the way "When Love Breaks Down" by Prefab Sprout, "True Faith" by New Order, or "Lips Like Sugar" by Echo and the Bunnymen, can.

"Tiger, Tiger" is a little-known instrumental by Duran Duran. When I was fourteen, they were without a doubt my favourite band. Yet when I listened to that song, I forgot who made it. It just seemed to exist, the way the stars in the sky existed.

I would lie there, my mind empty, my chest swelling with emotion... Joy? Sadness? It didn't matter. I was so much more than just this body and these thoughts. I felt connected to something greater than myself. I was part of the Great Chain of Being. I was Life itself!

I once played that song 27 times in a row at full volume, lying on my bed, my head in that timeless space...no beginning, no end, no Rina. Just the music and the feeling that I was everything and I was also nothing. Really...who needs drugs?

By the twenty-eighth time, Ton nearly threw my tape deck out the window.

"Tiger, Tiger" aside, I loved Duran Duran for purely shallow reasons. I was besotted after seeing the "Rio" video where Simon Le Bon cavorts around in his golden tan and black speedos.

I developed an obsession for all things Duran. I must've listened to each of their songs a thousand times.

Then I heard "So" by Peter Gabriel, whose husky crooning left me weak at the knees. I decided Sting and his falsetto and Simon and his whine were like little boys next to Peter. God, I loved his voice! I still do.

I also started having crushes on real boys, mostly friends of my older brother.

Hey Rina.

Oh! Hi Butch!

I was nearing the end of a long, awkward stage of braces, big nose and bad hair. I was really shy around Ton's friends and would sneak fascinated peeks whenever they came to the house.

I finally wanted to be more girly, to grow my hair and nails and wear dresses. But I was so worried people would notice and call attention to it.

Oh well... here goes!

As usual, I could rely on the *titas* to make my fears come true.

Everyone, look at Rina, she's wearing a *skirt*!

Now she's a real girl!!

With my Tony Manero walk, goofy voice and big feet, I wondered if guys would ever find me attractive.

My classmates were really sweet.

Hey Rins... Angelo said he, Jiggs and Jovy saw you biking down University Avenue yesterday and that you have sexy legs.

Really?

I remember at one party I wore a green sweater and jeans skirt. I'd just come back from the beach with a tan and for once I did feel pretty.

I think Marc keeps staring at you!

Although it's been 20 years since I moved to North America, my classmates have all come out to my dad's wake. This means more to me than I can say.

Where is she? Where's Rina??

?

My friend Tisha runs into the room and stares at me. We haven't seen each other in years.

I'm sorry. I am so sorry! Your dad was the best.

When we were growing up, Tisha was such a tomboy, more so than I.

She wore her hair as short as a boy and had big, clunky school shoes that looked like Doc Martens.

At fourteen, she was still flat-chested enough to get away with not wearing a bra.

These days, Tisha is married and the mother of two beautiful children.

She has certainly changed since our high school days when, like George in the "Famous Five" books by Enid Blyton, she was often mistaken for a boy.

Pare,* who's that guy being a bit too friendly with your sister? Do you want me to beat him up for you?

?

Idiot! That guy is a girl!

* Pronounced "Pa-reh" = "Dude" or "Bro" or "Man"

66

Tisha was as crazy about dogs as I was. In grade 4, she and I auditioned for the role of Sandy in a class production of "Annie".

WOOF! WOOF!

ARF! ARF!

"Annie" auditi... 4 PM

Rina, your barking is more realistic. You have the main role of Sandy and Tisha will be your understudy.

YESSS!

Tisha was one of those truly good people. She did not have a mean, calculating bone in her body.

Hiya Muffin! Hi Fuzzy!

Girls teased her about pretty much everything.

Hey Tish, what's with the combat boots?

They're huge. You look like a clown!

She ate the exact same lunch everyday -- chopped-up steak and rice.

Don't you ever eat anything else?

She never let anyone take a sip from her drink, no matter the pressure.

C'mon Tisha, what's the big deal? Oh so you're too good for us?

I just don't want to share germs.

She refused to change for P.E. class in front of the other girls.

Hey we're all girls here, you know. Why do you need to hide?

Tisha's not a real girl, remember?

Oh yeah! HA HA HA

In dignified fashion, she ignored the teasing. It seemed to me that she did not try to change for anyone. She also had the best manners of anyone I knew towards servants, and always spoke to them with respect.

Inday, time to take your bath.

Can't you see I'm busy reading?

Other girls

Inday, Tisha, time to take your bath.

Thank you Manang. I'll just finish this page.

Tisha

While my own *yaya* determined that I never dared show any other attitude except subservience towards her and the other helpers, unlike Tisha, my resulting meekness was born not out of kindness but out of fear!

Rin, time to take your bath.

But Mooom! I'm still reading!

Inday Rina. In the bath. *NOW.*

:gulp: Yes, Yaya.

At sleepovers, we would draw comics, ride our bikes, and play gin rummy using a deck of cards decorated with different breeds of dogs.

It was 1984 when, during a particular sleepover, Tisha and I made meatballs out of ground beef and wheat germ for our dogs.

We baked them in the oven and Tisha filled a glass jar of these doggie treats for me to take home. My parents picked me up and we headed to Lola's house for Sunday dinner.

I hope Fritz likes 'em!

Thanks Tish! Bye!

That night dinner was late, and when we arrived, I could hear my *lola* giving hell to the kitchen staff.

Not even the potato soup is ready! Don't you know everyone is starving??

Der Fuhrer is on a warpath.

It was at the height of the protest movement against the Marcos government and the atmosphere at my *lola*'s house, just like the rest of the country, was filled with tension.

My dad's oldest brother was an economics minister on the Marcos cabinet, whose members were derogatorily nicknamed Marcos's "*tutas*"* by the opposition.

Marcos and his brood

This had already been a source of conflict in the family before the assassination, but following that and with all the evidence of corruption that kept surfacing, the clan was more politically divided than ever.

* *tutas* = puppies

My dad simply could not understand my uncle's reasons for staying with the KBL party and kept trying to convince him to leave.

...completely lost the foreign market at this point. And of course the tourism industry is all but dead...

I'd placed my jar of doggie treats on the table and my uncle saw them.

...borrowing more and more money from the IMF but if all the country's earnings are just going back to pay our enormous debt...

?

...apart from the financial issues, just the sheer immorality on all levels that has been taking place...

...don't know if it's out of some misguided sense of honor or loyalty but you are going down with a sinking ship...

!

Mmm!

Aghast, I watched him pop two more into his mouth, chewing with gusto.

Uh... Daddy? Tito Cidito is eating the treats I made for Fritz.

...

HA HA HA HA!

?

Things were moving swiftly across the country. Along with public protests, various political groups, both openly and behind the scenes, were plotting to unseat Marcos.

One of these groups was RAM (Reformed Armed Forces Movement), a covert organization created by disgruntled military officers.

RAM was secretly supported by Marcos's own Defense Minister Juan Ponce Enrile (in case things headed south), and increasingly it gathered more members from within the military and government.

As for the other opposition groups, Marcos still wielded such control over the country that the only way they could win the upcoming 1987 elections was to unify into one party. But who would lead it?

People were pressuring Cory Aquino, Ninoy's widow, to run for the presidency. She had no experience but was a prominent figure in the protest movements and already loved by the people. Many felt she was the one candidate who could unite the nation against Marcos.

With some misgivings but for a chance at true democracy, each party leader gave up their political ambitions and agreed to back Cory.

But Cory was reluctant. She told her supporters she would only run under two conditions.

① If you manage to collect one million signatures.

② If Marcos calls for snap elections.

It was obvious Cory did not want to run. The million signatures could be achieved. But Marcos calling a snap election? Impossible.

Crap! We're screwed...

THE CORY AQUINO FOR PRESIDENT MOVEMENT

Then on November 1985, Marcos was being interviewed on ABC's "This Week With David Brinkley".

Well I understand the opposition has been asking for an election...

I announce that I am ready to call a snap election.

Are there any catches, Mr. President?

I'm ready. I'm ready.

If these childish claims to popularity on both sides have to be settled, I think we better settle it by calling an election right now.

Woo hoo! Game on, Mr. Marcos!

Noe? Are you watching this?

It was completely unexpected. Cory bowed to the inevitability of her fate. By December 1985, her candidacy was officially announced, with Salvador "Doy" Laurel (Ninoy's boyhood friend, political ally and current leader of the opposition) running as her Vice-President.

CORY AQUINO

DOY LAUREL

January, 1986. The new year began the campaign in earnest. My parents spent evenings working on voters lists, pasting up campaign posters and attending seminars on polling duties in outgoing *barangays.**

*villages

Yellow was the official color of the Aquino-Laurel ticket. At rallies I had goosebumps as I saw masses of yellow marching on the street.

"Tie A Yellow Ribbon" played everywhere. Yellow streamers tied to telephone poles and trees fluttered with life as we drove by highways and country roads.

We kids made posters and my dad printed banners and stickers, which he plastered wherever he could.

CORY: A BRIGHT HOPE
MARCOS: A PROVEN FAILURE

By coincidence we had a canary yellow station wagon known as "The Banana". Even before the campaign it was recognizable by everyone we knew, and it became a mascot of sorts at the marches.

Hey look, it's The Mapa car.

My dad drove the Banana and blared "Tie A Yellow Ribbon" from our tape deck through a megaphone. Next to him, my mom proudly waved a big yellow campaign flag while we children leaned out the windows, flashing the "L" sign for "LABAN" (which means "fight") and chanting "Co-ry! Co-ry!"

Across the country,
Cory-mania was everywhere.

My dad flew south to campaign among the personne[l]
of our farms. Wherever he drove, every house on the
stretch of road that runs down the Eastern coastline
of Negros displayed Aquino-Laurel posters.

Their campaign banner caught the attention of folks by the
roadside, and outstretched arms flashed the
LABAN sign as they drove past.

Even fishermen out at sea frantically waved
their hands at their campaign car.

It turns out that workers at the farm had needed
no convincing ... they'd already decided to vote
for the Aquino-Laurel ticket!

People flashed the "LABAN" sign across the country.

Index fingers pointed up in victory. Fists clenched, not with rage, but with purpose as thumbs extended out, open to change.

It was a gesture that at once combined hope with action.

It was a peaceful campaigning period in general. In a rare case of violence, a LABAN campaign manager in Tarlac was gunned down together with his driver.

BLAM BLAM BLAM

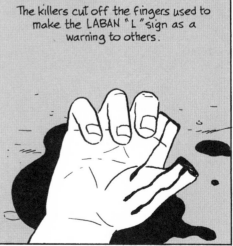

The killers cut off the fingers used to make the LABAN "L" sign as a warning to others.

Even at school, normally a politics-free zone, things got tense. The majority of my classmates were for Cory, but there were a few whose families remained loyal to Marcos.

CORY
← MARCOS →

I was very vocal in my disdain for the KBL party and didn't mince words.

Only an *idiot* would vote for Marcos!

A couple of girls fought back.

You know how much good President Marcos has done for our country?

Oh please. He's a crook. Everyone knows it.

But mostly they remained silent when we Cory supporters talked about marching in rallies. Each rally was like a party -- the more you went to, the cooler you were.

At times I got a little *too* vocal and passionate about the cause.

It's obvious that anyone still supporting Marcos is being *bribed!*

I forgot (or ignored) the fact that my cousin Tisa's dad was in the KBL party.

? SOB

In fact, the few Marcos supporters all had family who worked for the government.

Hey, what's up? Why're you crying?

Gina, who was the most fun-loving, easygoing, grinningest girl I knew, who never got mad at anyone, was yelling at me.

She's *crying* because you have such a *big mouth!*

But I was unapologetic. I believed this was a case of Good vs Evil.

But it's true!

Oh shut up. Can't you see how mean you're being?

I'M SO SICK OF CORY THIS AND CORY THAT. CAN'T WE JUST GO BACK TO HOW IT WAS??

I imagine it was like being the only Republican in a room full of smug, self-satisfied Democrats.

SOB

I told myself they were innocent bystanders in an awkward position. And besides, Tisa was one of my dearest friends. So I tried to be more careful after that.

No such care was needed around *lola* Loring, who, in her seventies, often joined in the rallies. After hearing her blistering tirades against Marcos I sure was relieved she was on our side.

I ♥ CORY

CORY

One of the largest rallies took place on Ayala Avenue, the heart of Manila's financial district.

CORY DOY

CORY DOY

CORY DOY

After marching with the massive crowds, we went inside to tita Lally's condo. The view from above was breathtaking. My dad's eyes shone for days after.

Princess, you are witnessing history!

February 7, 1986. Election Day. Everyone was prepared for the worst. We knew Cory would win the people's vote, but how could those votes actually be counted when Marcos controlled the media, the civil servants, and even COMELEC, the organization appointed to tally results?

Tens of millions lined up for hours to cast their ballot. In history, there had never been such a turnout. 400,000 volunteers joined NAMFREL (the National Movement of Free Elections) to guard returns and ballot boxes, sometimes forming human barricades to guard against tampering.

By this time, the world had taken notice. Foreign correspondents and TV crews littered the scenes. Incredibly, brazenly -- as though no one was watching -- Marcos thugs ran the gamut in their efforts to steal the vote, using bribery, threats, intimidation and violence.

Marcos wasn't concerned that the international media was witnessing everything. He knew he had the U.S. government firmly on his side.

For years the U.S. administration had turned a blind eye to the corruption and dictatorship in what was supposed to be a "democracy". After all, they had military bases to maintain, bases strategically located to keep communism at bay.

Niñoy Aquino's party had advocated for the removal of the U.S. military in the Philippines, and his widow looked certain to implement those policies if she won. So it was in Reagan's best interests that Marcos stay in power.

Besides which, the Marcoses and Reagans were as cosy as could be, with the same deluded sense of self-appointed grandeur and penchant for lavishness off the backs of the poor without harboring a speck of guilt.

Marcos had been openly committing theft, coercion and the abuse of human rights for decades, with no consequences. Election fraud was nothing. He and his buddy Ronnie would probably have a chuckle over it at their next soiree.

But unknown to Marcos, after the 1983 assassination, opinions about him changed among many U.S. officials. They now felt a Marcos regime was risking a spreading communist insurgency in a constantly weakened economy.

Behind the scenes, a group of them formed to explore ways of getting rid of Marcos and the instability he represented. Over the next two years, they tried to persuade Reagan to persuade Marcos to leave office.

Without taking further action, this group kept a close watch on Marcos. But when he announced snap elections on live TV, the American politicians were as surprised as anyone.

I'm ready. I'm ready.

Well well, son of a bitch...

And so it was that an official delegation of American observers sent to the Philippines by Reagan joined about a thousand foreign correspondents to witness the drama of the election unfold.

They witnessed KBL thugs beating people up in front of TV cameras and attempting to steal returns with strong arm tactics, the kind used by bullies to intimidate without actually shedding blood.

But Filipinos were tired of being bullied.

This time people fought back against every incident of threat, harrassment and cheating.

It was a valiant effort, but as the nation waited for their votes to be counted, there was a sinking feeling that all their best efforts would not be enough.

The Lord detests liars
PROV. 12:22

80

Marcos's reach proved too wide. On Feb. 15, the National Assembly declared him the winner, and it looked depressingly like it would be dictatorship deja-vu all over again.

As fate would have it, a series of events kept this from happening.

First, a group of young computer technicians from COMELEC who had witnessed the fraud firsthand, staged a dramatic walkout of their building in protest.

Then, 43-year-old Evelio Javier, one of the most promising opposition leaders, was assissinated. This sent new waves of outrage across the nation.

Next, the Catholic Bishops of the Philippines issued a statement condemning the election results. It was an unprecedented move.

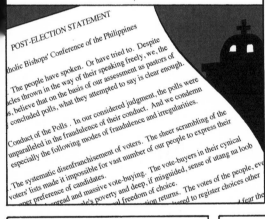

POST-ELECTION STATEMENT

Catholic Bishops' Conference of the Philippines

The people have spoken. Or have tried to. Despite obstacles thrown in the way of their speaking freely, we, the ... bishops, believe that on the basis of our assessment as pastors of ... the concluded polls, what they attempted to say is clear enough.

Conduct of the Polls . In our considered judgment, the polls were unparalleled in the fraudulence of their conduct. And we condemn especially the following modes of fraudulence and irregularities.

. The systematic disenfranchisement of voters. The sheer scrambling of the voters' lists made it impossible for vast number of our people to express their ... preference of candidates. The vote-buyers in their cynical ... spread and massive vote-buying. The vote-buyers in their cynical ... 's poverty and deep, if misguided, sense of utang na loob ... al freedom of choice.... tion returns. The votes of the people, eve ... ared to register choices other ... fear the

International governments refused to acknowledge Marcos as the winner, sending their congratulations to Cory instead. Filipinos began a mass boycott of banks and corporations owned by Marcos cronies and the stock market plummeted to record lows.

Pare, I just want this resolved so I can drink my San Miguel beer again!

Finally, Radio Veritas, the only station that was free from Marcos rule, announced Reagan's official statement, that the KBL party had "committed massive fraud".

Hah! Mr. Marcos, you can't hide behind Mr. Reagan any more!

It's about time!

Yet Marcos wouldn't relinquish power, even holding his own inauguration. After all, he had control over the Armed Forces. What could possibly happen to change that?

The answer came on Feb. 22, fifteen days after the elections. My parents were at a political meeting when...

Everyone! Breaking news on Radio Veritas!

Two of Marcos's right-hand men -- Defense Minister Enrile and Vice-Chief of Staff General Ramos -- had defected and barricaded themselves inside the Ministry of National Defense.

We do not consider President Marcos as being a duly constituted authority...

He has put his personal family interest above the interest of the people...

We are appealing to the other members of Cabinet to heed the will of the people expressed during the latest election...

We are here to take a stand. If any one of us will be killed... I think... all of us must be killed.

We'll stay here until we are all killed...

My God!

What now, Bishop?

I'm going to ask Cardinal Sin to make a general appeal to the Filipino people!

We must all support this revolution!

Tony, what can we do?

You heard the Bishop!

Thus my normally cautious, sensible parents and their friends impulsively headed into the eye of the storm: Camp Aguinaldo in the Ministry of National Defence.

GENERAL HEADQUARTERS
ARMED FORCES OF THE PHILIPPINES

They managed to enter with their vehicles just before the gates were ordered closed.

CLANG

Only then did they realize there was no turning back.

Hail Mary, full of grace, the Lord is with Thee...

Inside the camp, they were joined by reformist officers and their troops, journalists, some nuns, and a handful of civilians.

They were at the center of a *coup d'etat*, with no way of knowing how Marcos would respond to the rebellion.

Tony, how can our small group defend these guys against Marcos?

Hopefully more people will arrive.

My dad would soon get his wish. Cory and Butz Aquino, Ninoy's brother and a leader of the opposition, had spoken at length with the defectors and had decided to trust them. Now Butz himself was at Camp Aguinaldo.

We are here to try to prevent bloodshed.

... we will surround the camps and protect them with our bodies... we will do this because Enrile and Ramos wish to follow the will of the people...

I call on all our countrymen to join us and increase our numbers so that we can prevent a bloody confrontation.

Soon after, Cardinal Sin, the head of the church in the Philippines, made his own broadcast.

I am calling on our people to support our two good friends at the camp.

Pray to Our Lady that we will be able to resolve our problems peacefully.

It was 10pm. At this point, all of Metro Manila and the rest of the country were tuned in to Veritas.

Go to Camp Aguinaldo and show your solidarity with them in this crucial period.

It was what skeptical citizens of Manila needed -- endorsements from Cory and the Church itself! By midnight, crowds started to gather outside the gates of Aguinaldo.

Enrile had asked for food for his troops. If there is one thing Filipinos understand, it is the need for food at all times. And so food poured in.

My parents spent the next few hours of darkness helping to shuttle and distribute food to the troops.

Someone just brought one hundred hamburgers from Jolibee!

The next morning, people started filling EDSA, the ten-lane avenue flanked on either side by the two military camps that were housing the rebel troops.

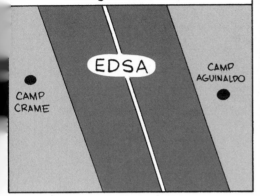

True to form, Filipinos treated the occasion like some kind of social gathering. Men, women and children of all ages brought blankets, radios and coolers full of food and drink, as though they were going for a picnic at Luneta Park.

So far, Marcos had been strangely slow to react to events. His Chief of Staff, General Ver, was occupied at a wedding the night before, and neither of them had been prepared for a scenario where a *coup d'etat* would be helped by ordinary Filipino citizens.

But now the word was out that Marcos had finally ordered his military to bring in the defectors, and the rebel leaders decided to consolidate their forces in one camp, Crame.*

* pronounced "*Krah-meh*"

As they crossed EDSA, soldiers were dumbstruck by the cheering crowds of people who had gathered to protect them.

At this point, my parents were able to leave Camp Aguinaldo and join the growing crowds that were now surrounding the perimeter of the camp.

People created barriers out of sandbags, fallen trees, parked cars and buses, but mostly of themselves.

In this way, almost every approach to Crame was blocked.

At 15h00, the first of the tanks started rolling in.

They were met by a sea of people from all walks of life...

...elderly Filipinos who were bedridden but insisted on being brought in their wheelchairs...

...families who brandished crucifixes, wielding statues of Our Lady as though they were shields...

...and young men armed with nothing more than t-shirts, jeans and *tsinelas*...

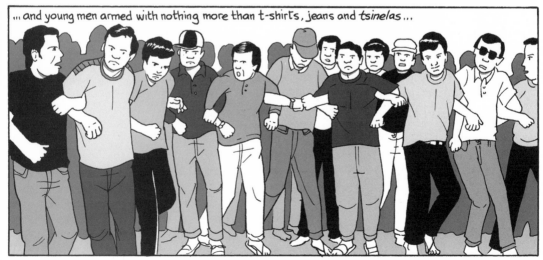

Before the world witnessed the events of China's Tiananmen Square, Filipino nuns placed themselves on the front lines and said the rosary as they faced down tanks.

While all this was going on, safe in our gated village of Ayala Alabang, Tonton was in a foul mood.

Why the hell didn't Mom and Dad bring me with them?!

History is being made and I'm stuck here with the babies!

Yo! We're not babies!

DING DONG

Oh... Hi Mike.

Hey Ton, a bunch of us are headed to General Ramos's house here in Alabang... to protect his family? You and Rina wanna come?

Cool! Let me just tell yaya Luz.

I just need to use the bathroom!

Omigod, maybe Butch will be there!

Or Billy...? He's always so nice to me...

PSSHH

Paco is so cute... but he doesn't even know I exist ...

HEY RASTAPOPOULOS! LET'S GO!

The General's house was only minutes away. When we got there, it looked like the entire village had had the same idea.

Cool...

89

It was our own mini EDSA.

Armoured vehicles with soldiers loyal to Ramos were stationed on the street.

Military helicopters flew overhead and foolishly we shouted and waved the *LABAN* sign at them.

Back at EDSA (where, let's be honest, the real danger lay) the crowds outside the camp had grown from five hundred at sunrise to over half a million by midday.

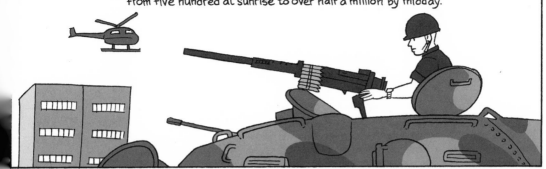

In the end, not even the most jaded, battle-hardened soldiers could bring themselves to fire on old women in wheelchairs, or on kneeling nuns. Or on children.

As tanks and APCs were repeatedly blocked by people willing to die to protect the rebels, Marcos troops, non-plussed, began defecting on the spot.

Soldiers who were handed garlands of flowers by smiling girls obligingly draped them around their machine guns.

One general was not happy.

I have my orders! Disperse now!

Word spread and soon a caller phoned Radio Veritas, wanting to speak to the general. His message was blared on loudspeaker.

Arturo, this is your tito Fred speaking.

Your tita Florence and I and all your cousins are here in Crame... now boy, please listen to me...

Halt the tanks.

YAAAAY!

Veritas was the only radio station free from Marcos rule. Earlier that day, it had been raided and neutralized by Ver's men. But it popped up again, operating in clandestine fashion at a secret makeshift location less than one kilometer from Marcos's residence, Malacañang Palace.

CLOSED
TRANSMITTERS TOTALLY WRECKED!

For much of the weekend, Veritas was solely manned (or "wo-manned") by broadcaster June Keithley, her technician, and two teenage boys named Paolo and Gabe Mercado.

Veritas became a tool to link the rebel leaders with the opposition and church leaders and the people of EDSA. Tactical plans and defensive strategies were relayed by General Ramos to Keithley, who made live broadcasts to the crowds. In this way, incoming Marcos troops were continuously blocked by an organised People Power.

June, I've received word that 3 six-by-sixes...

...and two APCs full of soldiers are nearing Guadalupe Bridge.

You heard the General, everyone...

...all nearby vigilantes, please head there at once.

LET'S GO!

All that day, troops were defecting, and Ramos and Enrile were exhilarated.

WELCOME DEFECTION CENTER

But in the early hours before dawn, Marcos announced he was sending in his Marines and launching a full assault strike by land and by air.

Well, this could be it. If there are any foreigners here, I suggest you inform your embassies.

Villamor Air Base, 5:15 AM. Colonel Sotelo, Commander of the 15th Strike Wing, briefed his men on their mission: to fly their aircraft straight into the rebel stronghold.

Meanwhile, on the ground approaching Crame...

RRRUMMBLE

Lord, you know that there are many people out there...

"YOU KNOW WHAT WE ARE GOING THROUGH RIGHT NOW.

"THERE ARE MANY OF US AND WE ARE TRYING TO DO OUR DUTY.

"WE ASK YOU TO PLEASE GUIDE US, LORD.

"YOU ASK US TO ALWAYS TURN THE OTHER CHEEK.

"WE ASK YOU NOW TO SHOW US THAT TRULY NOTHING GOOD CAN COME FROM EVIL."

"SHOW US, LORD, THAT ONLY GOOD WILL WORK IN THIS WORLD.

"PLEASE TAKE CARE OF ALL WHO ARE OUT THERE. PROTECT THEM AND SAVE THEM FROM HARM.

"THERE ARE CHILDREN OUT THERE, YOUNG GIRLS AND BOYS, PARENTS, BROTHERS AND SISTERS, HUSBANDS AND WIVES.

"WHO KNOWS WHAT THEY MAY HAVE TO FACE THIS MORNING?

"WE ADD OUR PRAYERS TO THE PRAYERS OF THE PEOPLE IN OUR COUNTRY."

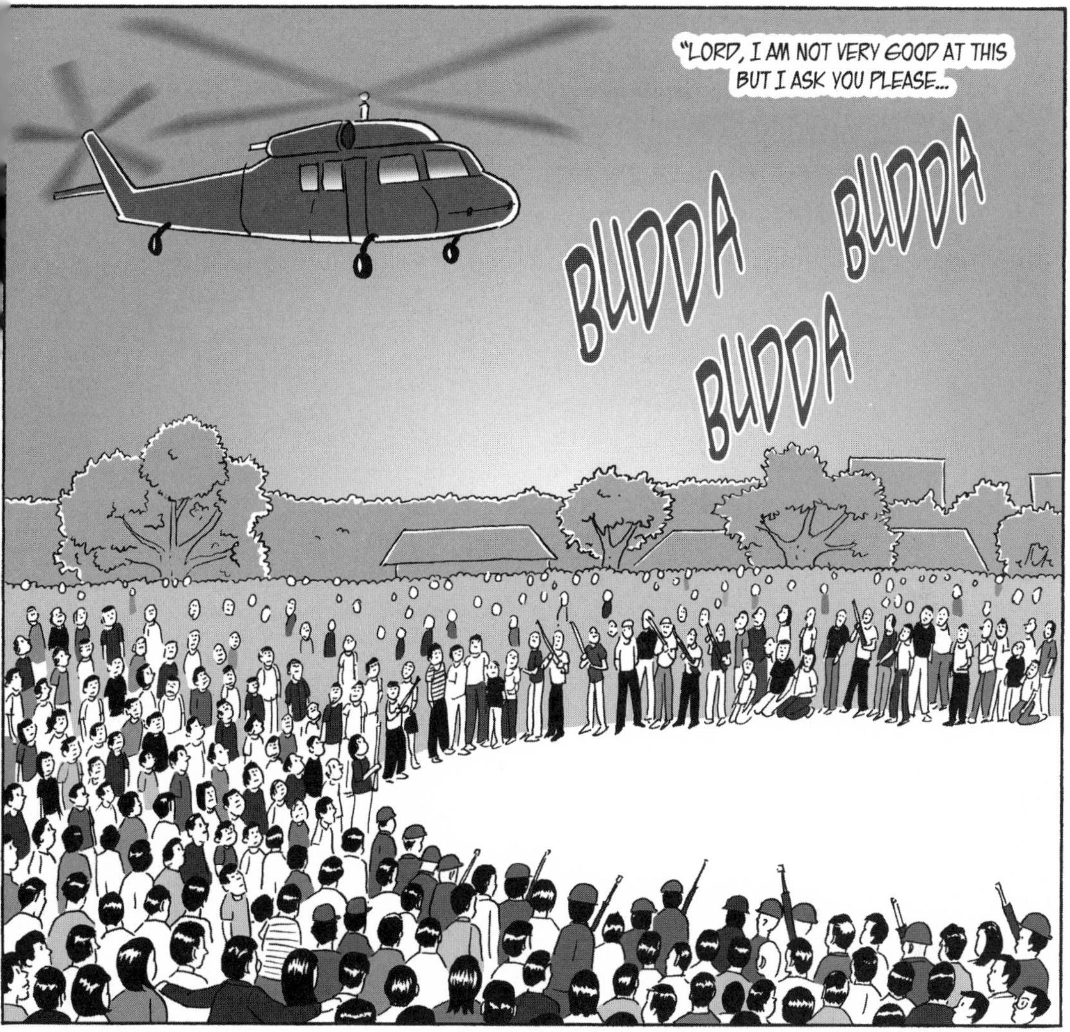
"LORD, I AM NOT VERY GOOD AT THIS BUT I ASK YOU PLEASE...
BUDDA BUDDA BUDDA

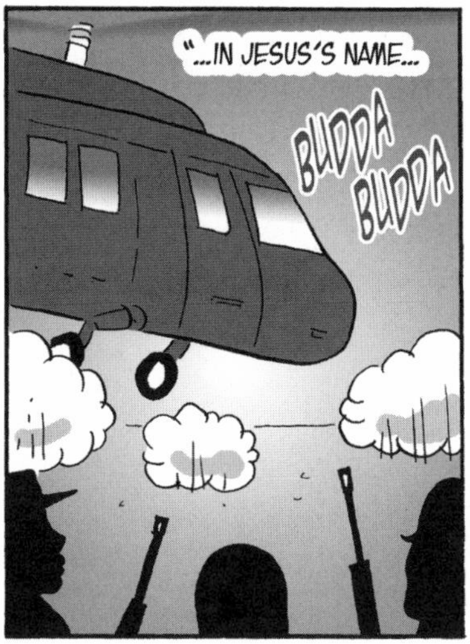
"...IN JESUS'S NAME...
BUDDA BUDDA

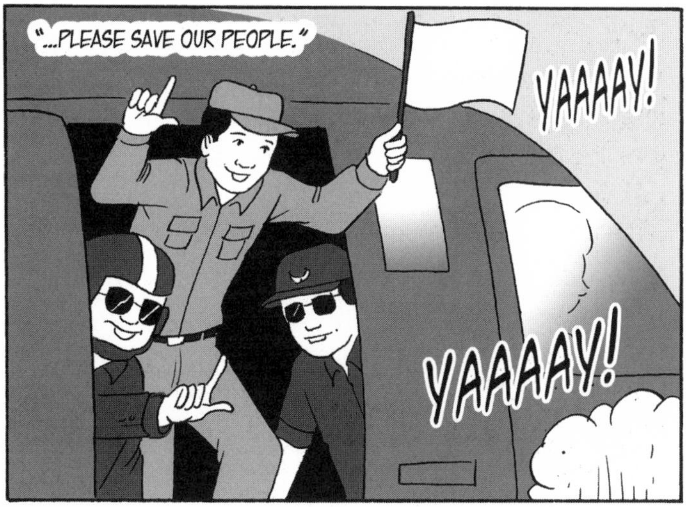
"...PLEASE SAVE OUR PEOPLE."
YAAAAY!
YAAAAY!

After that major defection, the rest of the Armed Forces followed. By Monday morning, four days after the first defection, it was all over. Marcos and his entourage fled by helicopter to Hawaii, where Reagan granted them political asylum.

The Manila Times
MARCOS FLEES
BAP to keep national five
Family, Ver off with FM
Cory Installed

Across the country, jubilant Filipinos celebrated the return to democracy.

CHINA ARTS
MERCURY DRUG
METROBAN
CORY

Malacañang Palace was ransacked and looted. Imelda's 3,000 pairs of shoes were discovered. Unfortunately, a legend was born.

A proper inauguration for Cory was attended by the men of the hour, Ramos and Enrile, truly a startling turn of events.

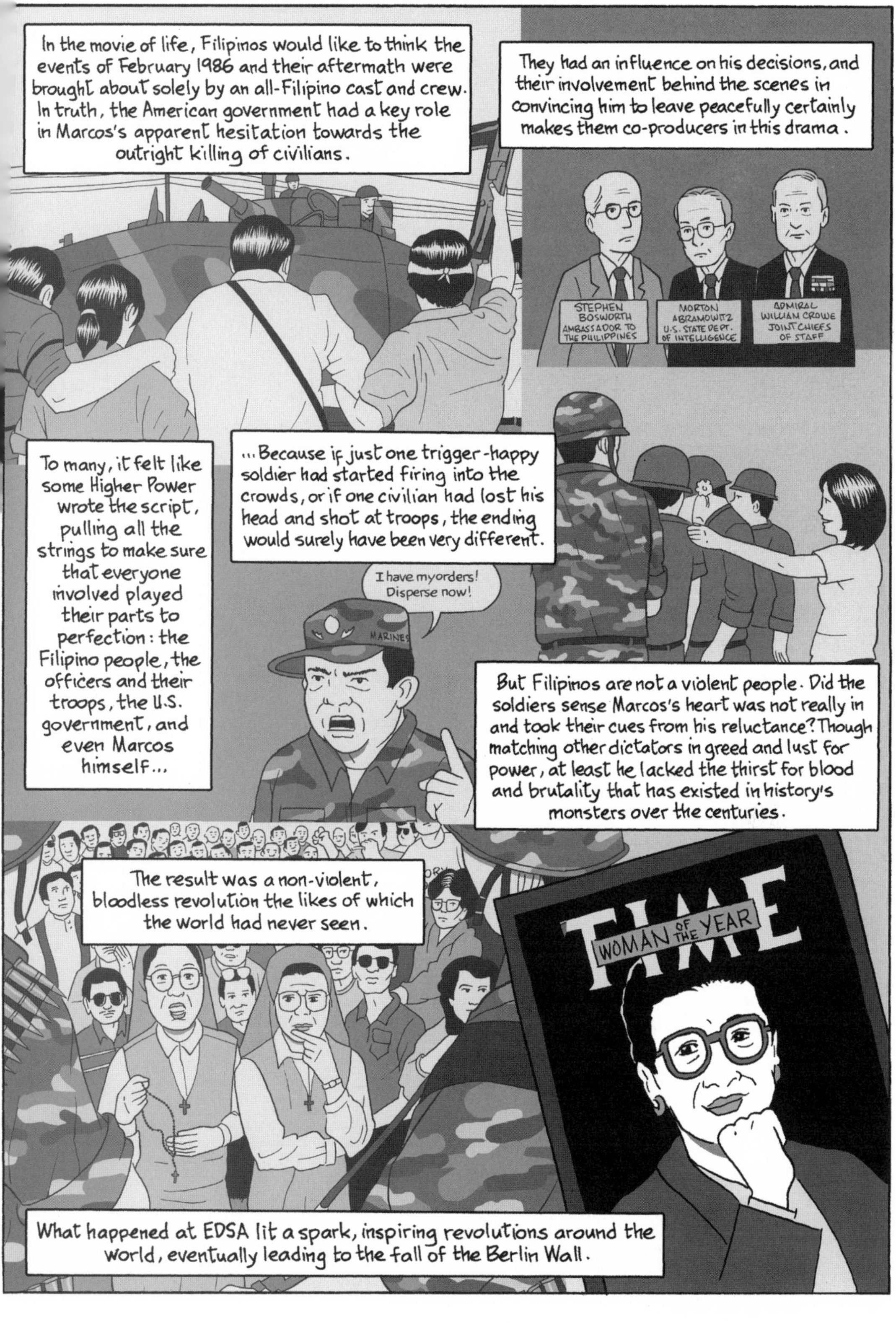
In the movie of life, Filipinos would like to think the events of February 1986 and their aftermath were brought about solely by an all-Filipino cast and crew. In truth, the American government had a key role in Marcos's apparent hesitation towards the outright killing of civilians.
They had an influence on his decisions, and their involvement behind the scenes in convincing him to leave peacefully certainly makes them co-producers in this drama.
STEPHEN BOSWORTH AMBASSADOR TO THE PHILIPPINES
MORTON ABRAMOWITZ U.S. STATE DEPT. OF INTELLIGENCE
ADMIRAL WILLIAM CROWE JOINT CHIEFS OF STAFF
To many, it felt like some Higher Power wrote the script, pulling all the strings to make sure that everyone involved played their parts to perfection: the Filipino people, the officers and their troops, the U.S. government, and even Marcos himself...
...Because if just one trigger-happy soldier had started firing into the crowds, or if one civilian had lost his head and shot at troops, the ending would surely have been very different.
I have my orders! Disperse now!
MARINES
But Filipinos are not a violent people. Did the soldiers sense Marcos's heart was not really in and took their cues from his reluctance? Though matching other dictators in greed and lust for power, at least he lacked the thirst for blood and brutality that has existed in history's monsters over the centuries.
The result was a non-violent, bloodless revolution the likes of which the world had never seen.
TIME
WOMAN OF THE YEAR
What happened at EDSA lit a spark, inspiring revolutions around the world, eventually leading to the fall of the Berlin Wall.

The Aquino government assigned my dad as Cultural Attaché to North America. Four months after the revolution, we moved to Washington D.C.

Ironically, now that the dictatorship they wanted to leave behind was no longer there, my parents plans to emigrate came true after all.

MABUHAY
MARCOS
ERAP CORY
GLORIA RAMOS

Jollibee

It's 2:30 AM and I can't sleep. The cremation and funeral are in a few hours' time.

I'm supposed to write a eulogy. I can't think of what to say.

My dad and *tito* Dave were football (soccer) fans. I remember how, when the World Cup was on, they tried to watch the games live via satellite. Because of the time difference in hosting nations, games were often shown at ungodly hours. My dad would wake me and Ton up in the middle of the night and we'd drive to tito Dave's house to watch a match between Germany and Brazil at three in the morning.

Yahoo! No traffic!

That only took 15 minutes!

YAWN

C'mon guys. The game's started!

Our cousins Paul and Claudine were already awake and waiting for us.

Today, I am a rabid football fanatic. I watch, I coach and I play. I follow all the transfer news and know who's who in the different leagues in Europe.

These days when I start chatting about football with other fans (usually men), they are taken aback by how much I actually know.

I'm a Liverpool supporter.

Oh, too bad Suarez is headed for Barcelona. But I'm curious to see how Adam Lallana will fit in.

As I continue to discuss Bayern Munich's recent dominance in the Champions League and whether Jose Mourinho is a tactical genius or an egotistical maniac (verdict: he's both), the men stare at me, confused that this little Asian woman knows more about football than they do.

???

I really wish Toni Kroos had gone to Man U. I mean, Real Madrid already have James Rodriguez, C.Ronaldo, Benzema ... Gareth *Bale*, for heaven's sake. Yes, Kroos is a mid, but that's just being greedy ...

When I coach recreational soccer, in my head I look like a middle-aged white man from the English Premiere League. So I'm always surprised when players don't respond to me as such.

We'll go with a traditional 4-4-2 and use the center back as a sweep just ahead of the full back.

Hey boys, are you listening?

As for playing, here's what tends to happen when I miss a game due to other commitments.

Santa Claus Parade

School Barbecue

Nephew's birthday

At the 1998 World Cup, Brazil was playing France in the finals in Paris. It was a sunny afternoon in Montreal as I sat down for the kick-off. Half a world away in Manila, my dad was watching in the bleary hours after midnight.

Allez Les Bleus!

I had become a huge Zinedine Zidane fan and earlier over the phone I'd told my dad I had a feeling France would win.

Against Brazil?? Impossible!

Yes they will! You'll see! Zidane will come up with some magic!

I don't think so, Princess.

Zidane!

LA POSTE

BRA 0 | FRA 1

Yessss!! Go Zizou!!

Powerful header by Zinedine Zidane! France lead with 27 minutes gone...

Hey Babe! France just scored!

That's nice!

103

RRRRING!

Hello?

?

Hello?

Who was that, Rina?

I don't know. Whoever it was hung up.

ZIDANE AGAIN! And again, Brazil looking poor defensively on the set piece... it's 2-nil France.

BRA FRA
0 - 2

YESSSS!

RRRRING!

Hello? Hello?

Heh heh... I know who it is!

Was that the phone again?

I think it's my dad. He's ringing every time France scores!

CHAK

Oookay...

When Daniel and I were having a long-distance relationship between New Jersey and Montreal, to save money, we only called each other twice a week.

So Daniel thought of a way to say goodnight to me at the end of each day. He would ring me at 10:00 pm, just once, then hang up.

RRRING

I would ring back once and hang up too.

RRRING

We did this whenever I went to the Philippines without him.

RRRING!

I'll get that.

?

No Mom, leave it! It's 10 o'clock. Daniel's just ringing to say goodnight.

At the time, long-distance rates were $1.20 a minute

See? Now I ring back once and then hang up.

I see!

RRING
PEEP!

To my dad, who was a romantic as well as cheap, this was a stroke of genius.

That is so sweet, Princess!

I know! Right?

Blecch!

Petit continues his run which started from the back... AND HE SCORES! And gives France the perfect finish...

BRA	FRA
0	3

It's a total celebration in the Stade de France... the hosts have won the World Cup in style...

Yesss! France just scored again! You'll see, the phone will ring!

Sure enough...

RRRRING!

Sporting events turned into a sort of code between me and my dad, an excuse to ring each other. He was a Tiger Woods fan; we loved it when he won a tournament just so we could ring each other and hang up.

...and Tiger has just putted for birdie to win the U.S. Open!

RRRING!

Yahoo!

" ...it's Princess! "

≥SOB≤

Why??

RRRING!!

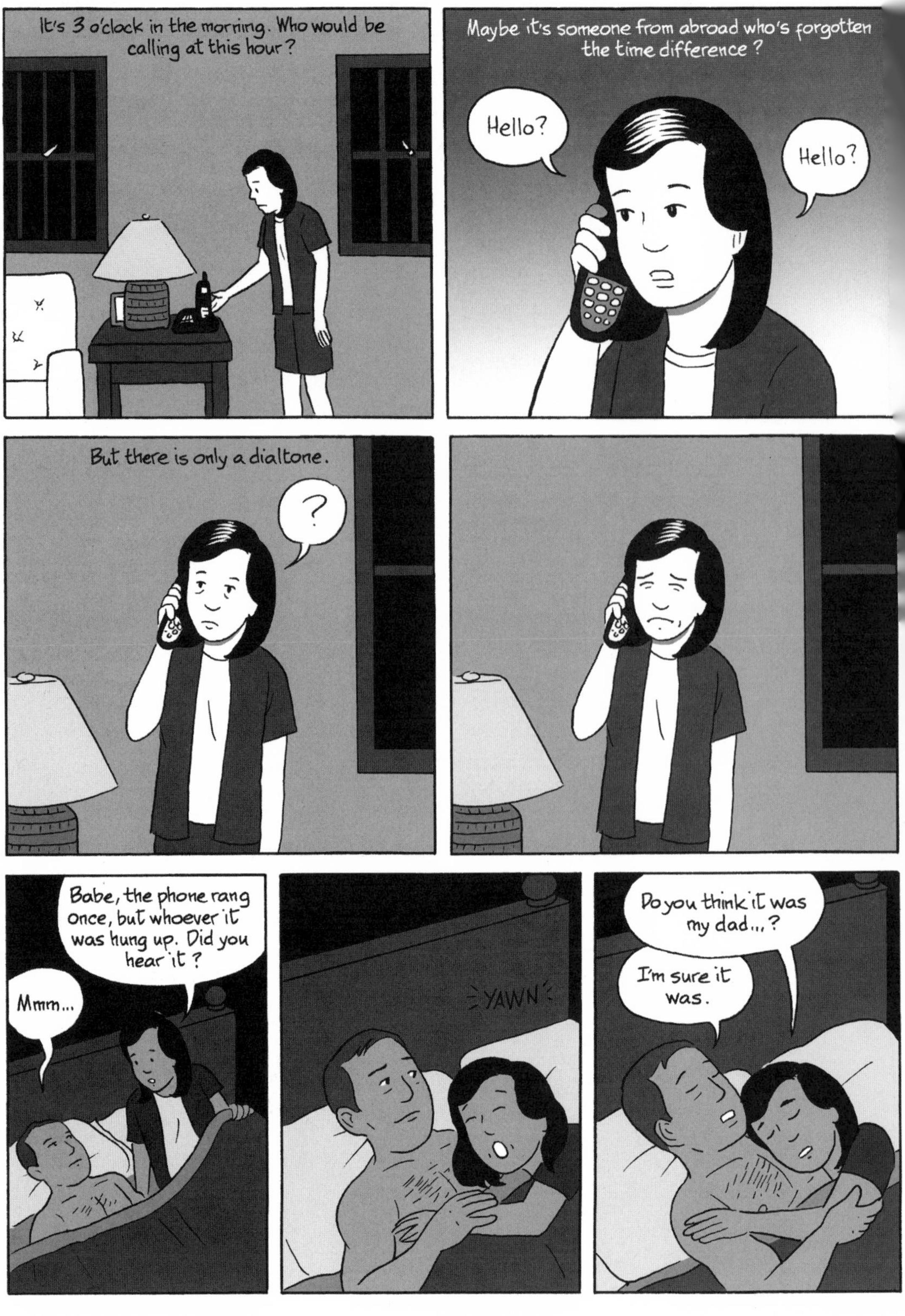
It's 3 o'clock in the morning. Who would be calling at this hour?
Maybe it's someone from abroad who's forgotten the time difference?
Hello?
Hello?
But there is only a dialtone.
?
Babe, the phone rang once, but whoever it was hung up. Did you hear it?
Mmm...
YAWN
Do you think it was my dad...?
I'm sure it was.

The summer of 1986 would end up being my last one in the Philippines, and I did all the usual things I'd always done, except that every day was as vivid to me as to someone taking in a place they knew they would never see again.

So I borrowed the Adrian Mole books from Gina and watched John Hughes films with Suzette and Chinie. I biked up and down the wide open streets of Ayala Alabang and went to parties where my friends played OMD's "If You Leave" and "Don't You Forget About Me" by the Simple Minds and wrote me sweet letters of goodbye.

All the while, I felt I was looking at everything through some kind of strange lens, as though I were the only thing real and all around me was just a movie...

...as though I was trying to separate myself from this world so it wouldn't hurt to leave it.

Last night...
was that real?

What *is* real?

'Morning, Nicholas. Lolo's funeral is later today. Here, you can wear this shirt.

It's so hot. Can I just wear short sleeves?

Okay, sure.

When Nicholas was little, my dad was able to visit us often because of his business trips. Nicholas was his first grandchild, and they adored each other.

I see you Wowo!

Yahoo!

...and Peterbilt, and Tonko twuck, and Mack twuck...

Wow! You sure know your trucks!

You want banana?

But Nicholas has yet to shed a tear since learning of the accident.

He seems a curious, distant observer of it all.

Rina, Daddy's body will be cremated now, but Mom won't be watching. It will be too much for her. Are you coming?

No, I... I guess I'll just stay here with Mom.

Okay. See you.

Have you seen Nicholas?

I'm sure he's around somewhere. Why?

"I'm worried he might be watching the cremation."

Mommy??

Poor Lolo! Why did they have to *burn* him ??

So you *did* see the cremation...

Poor Lolo!

⸎SOB⸎

The floodgates have opened.

⸎SOB⸎
⸎SOB⸎

After the funeral, Daniel and Nicholas fly back to Canada a few days before my own departure.

I'm able to spend time with my mom before I head home.

On my trip back, I have mixed feelings.

I'm sad about leaving my mom. I feel strange about traveling without my husband and son.

But I'm also grateful for the solitude. Now I don't have to worry about anyone but myself.

I'm just a passenger on a plane.

I can forget everything.

At customs, the forgetting comes to an end.

And what was the purpose of your visit to Manila?

My dad's funeral...

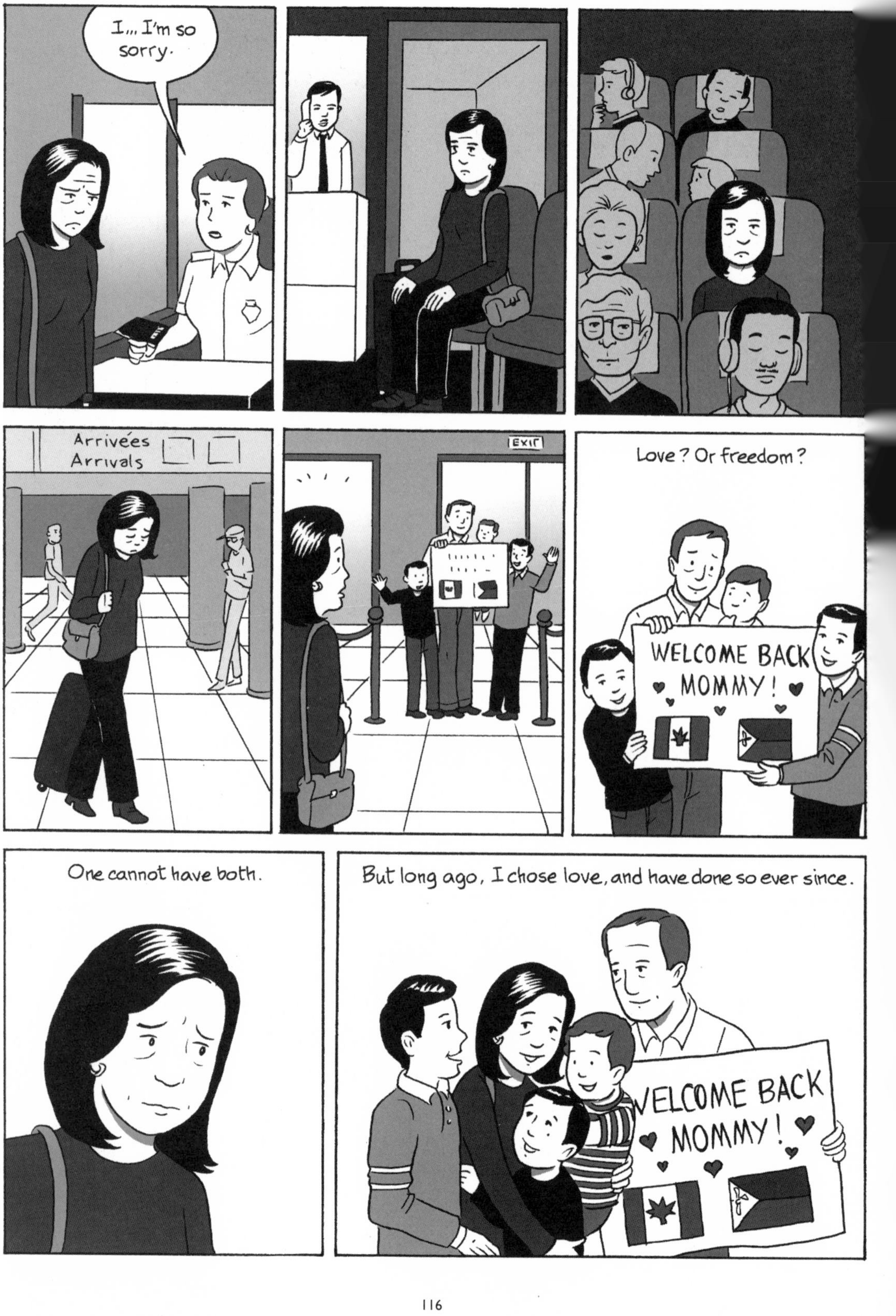
I... I'm so sorry.
Arrivées
Arrivals
EXIT
Love? Or freedom?
WELCOME BACK MOMMY!
One cannot have both.
But long ago, I chose love, and have done so ever since.
WELCOME BACK MOMMY!

Some months later, Mia is born, a perfect, beautiful little girl. Our family is complete.

Life goes on, a non-stop blur of child-rearing, work, school and activities. As each day spills dizzyingly into the next, there is no time to think.

I can almost pretend my dad is still alive since I hadn't seen him that often to begin with. I use a technique when dealing with painful situations which is: I simply think about something else.

It's taken me a long time to get over not having my family around me -- my parents, siblings, my cousins whom I'd grown up with. I see them from time to time but it is so different from them being part of our everyday life and with me on birthdays, Christmases, weekend lunches -- the kind of things most people take for granted.

There is a constant ache, a loneliness that you can't understand unless you've been there.

One month I'll email and check out Facebook daily, the next month I won't be in touch with anyone at all. I find when I have less contact, I grow used to the lack of connection, and missing everyone becomes a dull pang of regret that I am able to push aside.

I fall into bed each night exhausted from feedings, endless household chores, taking the kids to their hockey, swimming, karate, piano lessons, doctor and dentist appointments, homework, school meetings, coaching two soccer teams while playing myself, and of course, work. Every minute of the day is a blessed distraction.

But the things you try to hide from eventually have their way of coming out.

iMac

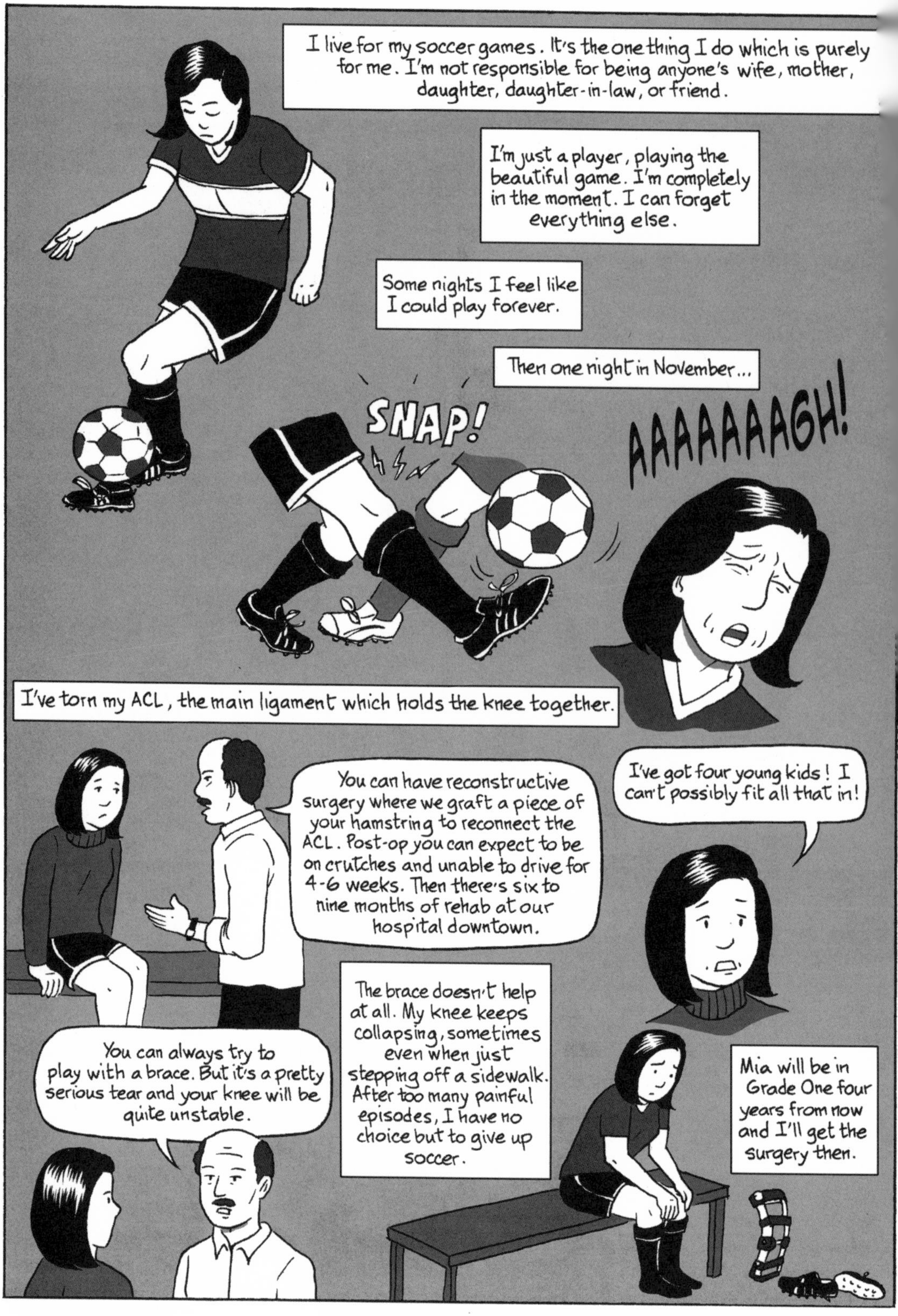

I live for my soccer games. It's the one thing I do which is purely for me. I'm not responsible for being anyone's wife, mother, daughter, daughter-in-law, or friend.
I'm just a player, playing the beautiful game. I'm completely in the moment. I can forget everything else.
Some nights I feel like I could play forever.
Then one night in November...
SNAP!
AAAAAAAGH!
I've torn my ACL, the main ligament which holds the knee together.
You can have reconstructive surgery where we graft a piece of your hamstring to reconnect the ACL. Post-op you can expect to be on crutches and unable to drive for 4-6 weeks. Then there's six to nine months of rehab at our hospital downtown.
I've got four young kids! I can't possibly fit all that in!
You can always try to play with a brace. But it's a pretty serious tear and your knee will be quite unstable.
The brace doesn't help at all. My knee keeps collapsing, sometimes even when just stepping off a sidewalk. After too many painful episodes, I have no choice but to give up soccer.
Mia will be in Grade One four years from now and I'll get the surgery then.

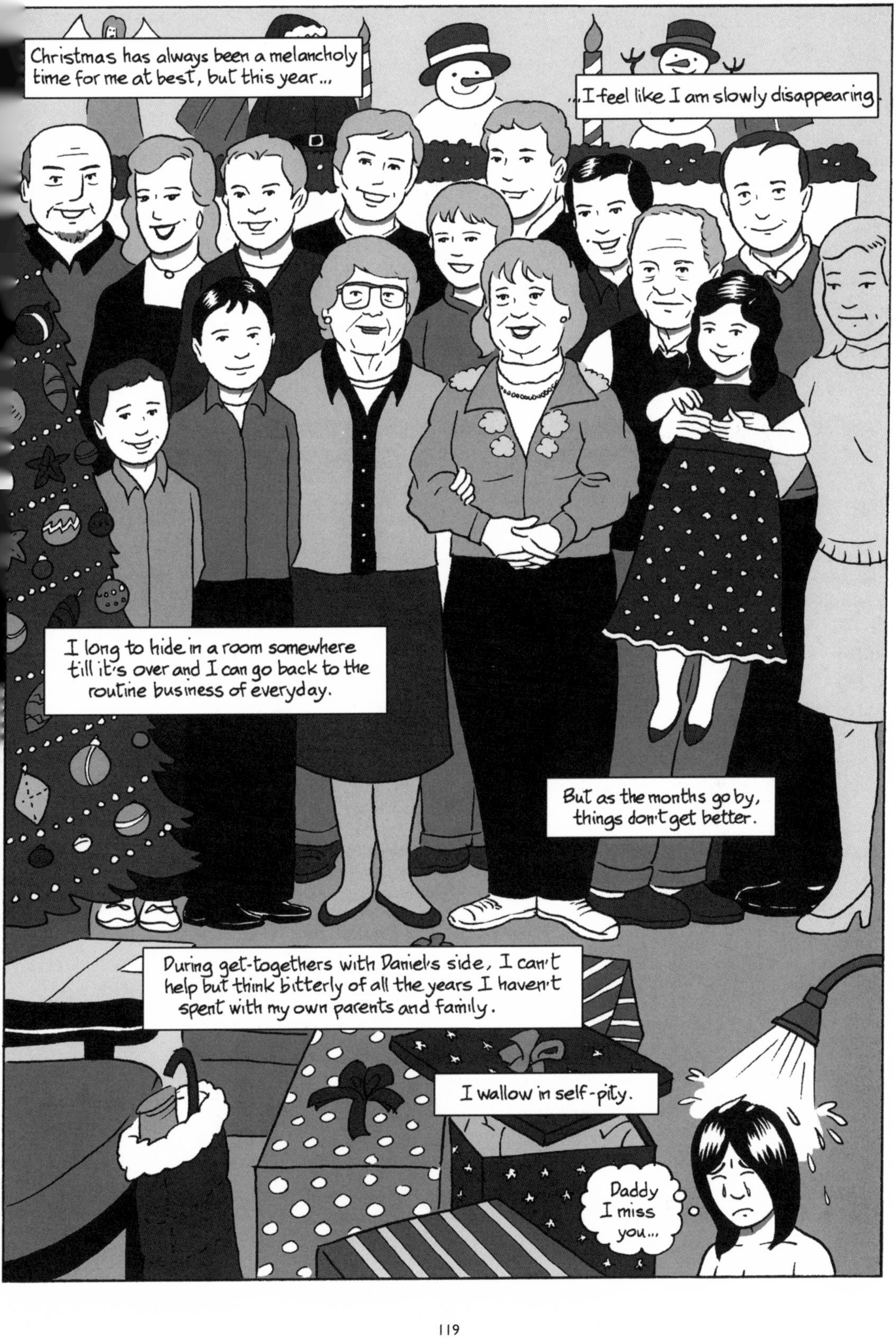
Christmas has always been a melancholy time for me at best, but this year...
...I feel like I am slowly disappearing.
I long to hide in a room somewhere till it's over and I can go back to the routine business of everyday.
But as the months go by, things don't get better.
During get-togethers with Daniel's side, I can't help but think bitterly of all the years I haven't spent with my own parents and family.
I wallow in self-pity.
Daddy I miss you...

One day, I am working on the computer, live-streaming the CBC, when...

Do you enjoy New Wave? Hi, I'm Jian Ghomeshi, the host of "Q". Welcome to the CBC's New Wave channel, with songs from my own personal collection.

I'M TAKING A RIDE WITH MY BEST FRIEND I HOPE HE NEVER LETS ME DOWN AGAIN PROMISES ME WE'RE AS SAFE AS HOUSES AS LONG AS I REMEMBER WHO'S WEARING THE TROUSERS I HOPE HE NEVER LETS ME DOWN AGAIN

Yesterday I got so old I felt like I could die Yesterday I got so old It made me want to cry Go on, go on Just walk away Go on, go on Your choice is made

SO IF YOU TAKE THEN PUT BACK GOOD IF YOU STEAL BE ROBIN HOOD IF YOUR EYYYYYYES ARE WANTING ALL YOU SEE THEN I THINK I'LL NAME YOU AFTER ME I THINK I'LL CALL YOU APPETITE

THESE THINGS THAT I'VE BEEN TOLD CAN REARRANGE MY WORLD MY DOUBT IN TIME BUT NOT INSIDE OUT THIS IS THE WORKING HOUR WE ARE PAID BY THOSE WHO LEARN BY OUR MISTAKES

Touch me how can it be Believe me The sun always shines on TV Ho-o-o-o-ld me close to your heart Touch me and give all your love to meeeee

I try to discover A little something to make me sweeter Oh baby refrain From breaking my hea-a-a-a-rt i'm so in love with you I'll be forever blue That you give me no reason Why you're making me work so hard

Oh baby PLEEEEEEASE Give a little RESPE-E-E-CT TO-O-O-O-O-O-O MEEEEEEEEEEEEE!

I haven't heard these songs in over 20 years!

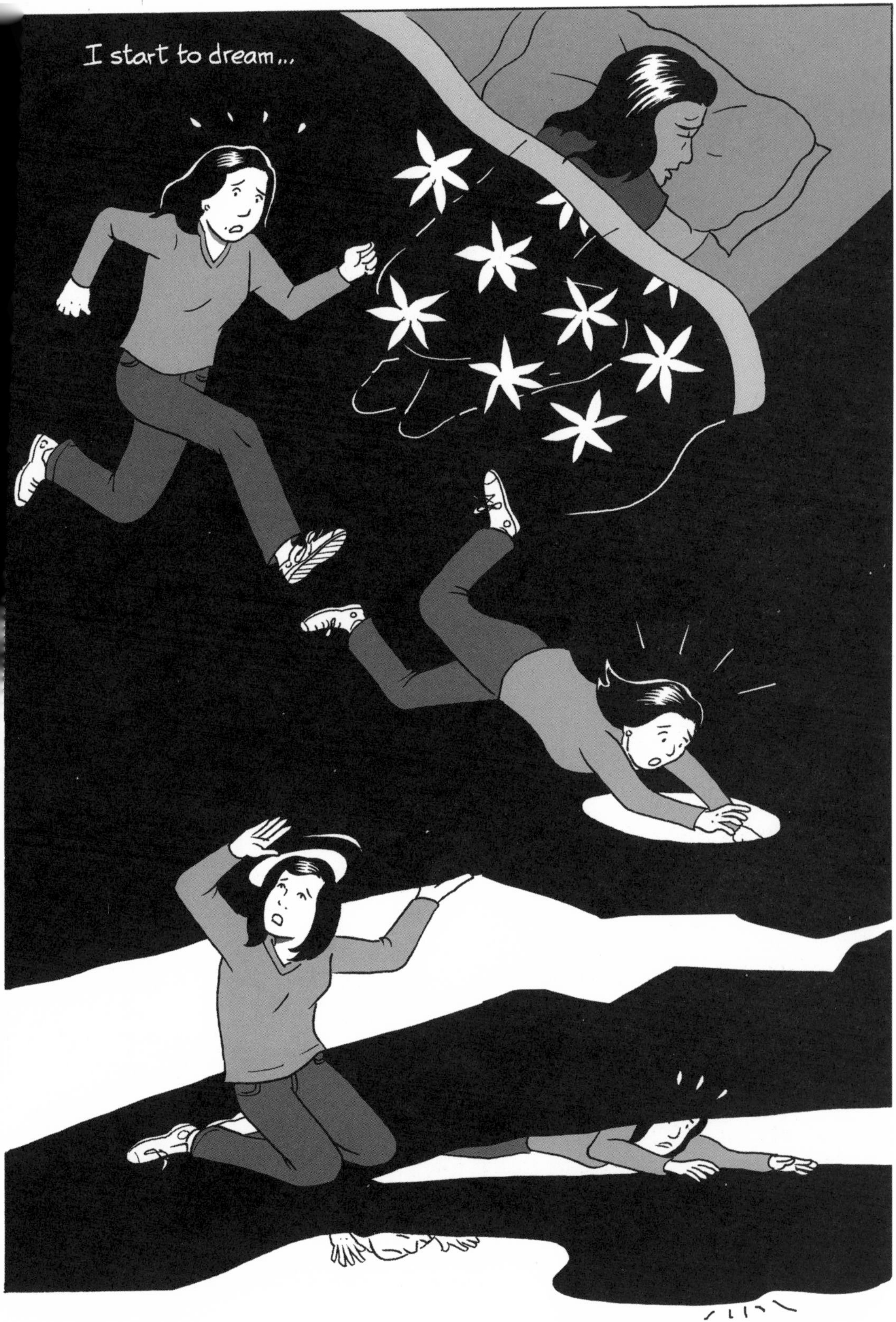
I start to dream...

One winter's day in February, Daniel takes the kids to his parents in the Eastern Townships for a weekend of skiing.

Wave bye to Mommy

It's a chance for me to work on my art portfolio. I've been busy developing websites and lettering English versions of Japanese manga. I haven't actually drawn anything in years.

I also haven't had a weekend all to myself in years.

Freedom!

BEEP

YAWN

One dish!

TINK
TINK

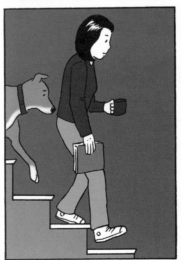

CLICK

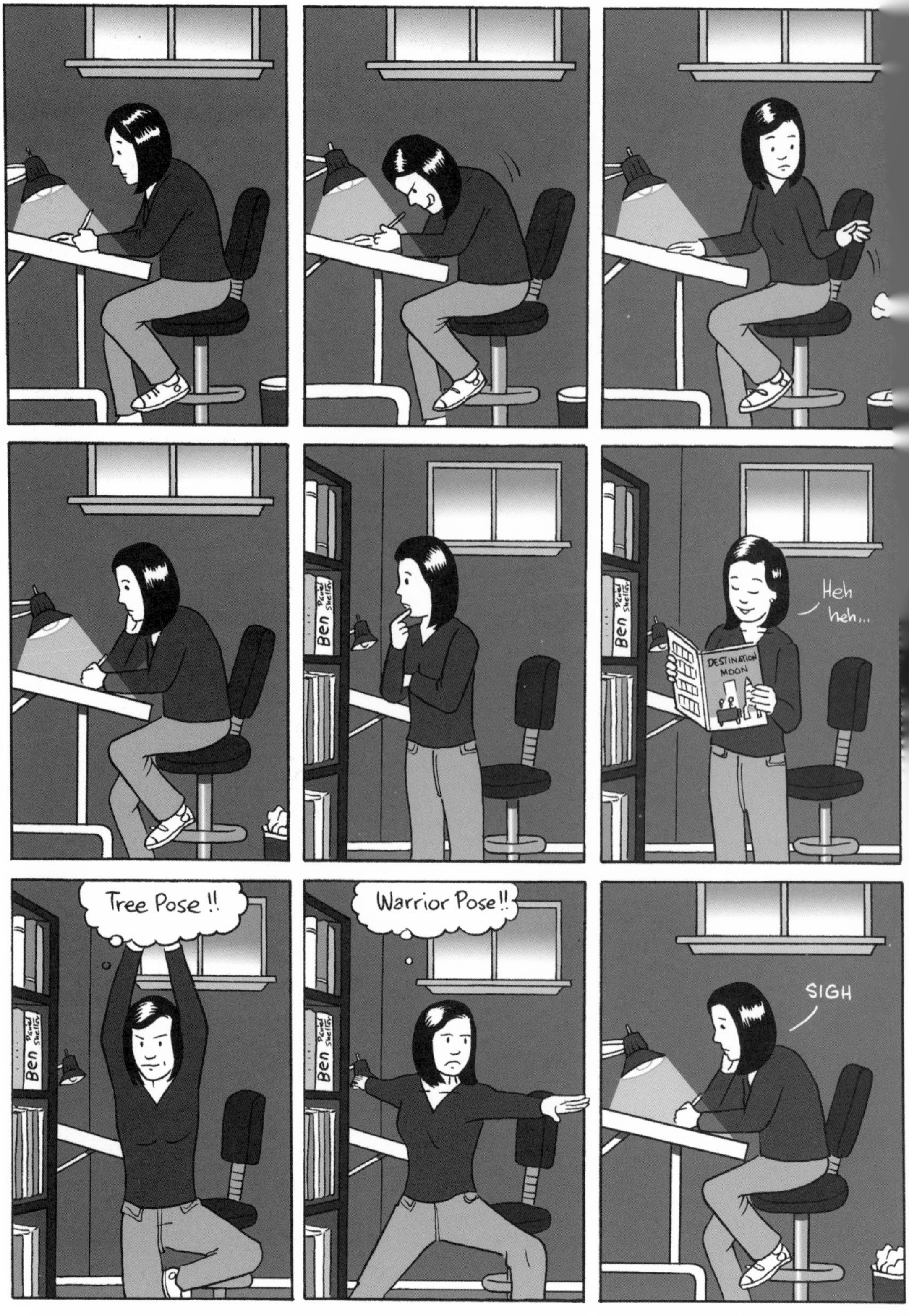
Ben
Percival Shelley
Heh heh...
DESTINATION MOON
Tree Pose!!
Warrior Pose!!
SIGH

give up and grab some dinner. I eat on the sofa while watching the Winter Olympics on TV.

I think of calling up my cousin for a long cozy chat or going out for coffee with a friend. But it is so rare I am by myself that I am relishing the solitude.

That night I read for four hours while snacking on sour cream and onion potato chips. Total heaven!

The next day I get serious. I start scribbling ideas for a children's book and do random sketches of people and animals.

But I am so rusty. Everything I draw seems stiff, with no style at all.

My stuff sucks... who am I kidding?

I'll never have a career as a true artist!

What's become of me?

Who am I??

Daniel and the kids will come home and I will be there on the outside but completely gone inside.

Uh... Babe?

I wonder what became of that girl who loved animals and New Wave, who drew comics and hung out with her cousins, who was fun-loving and generous and kind.

All that's left now is a 40-year old woman who yells constantly at her kids, who frets all day about work and chores and bills, who never manages to catch up with friends. Who is impatient and negative and mean. I have become all the things I never was before.

I think of my dad and am filled with regret. That little girl he loved so unconditionally is gone, and has probably been gone for years.

126

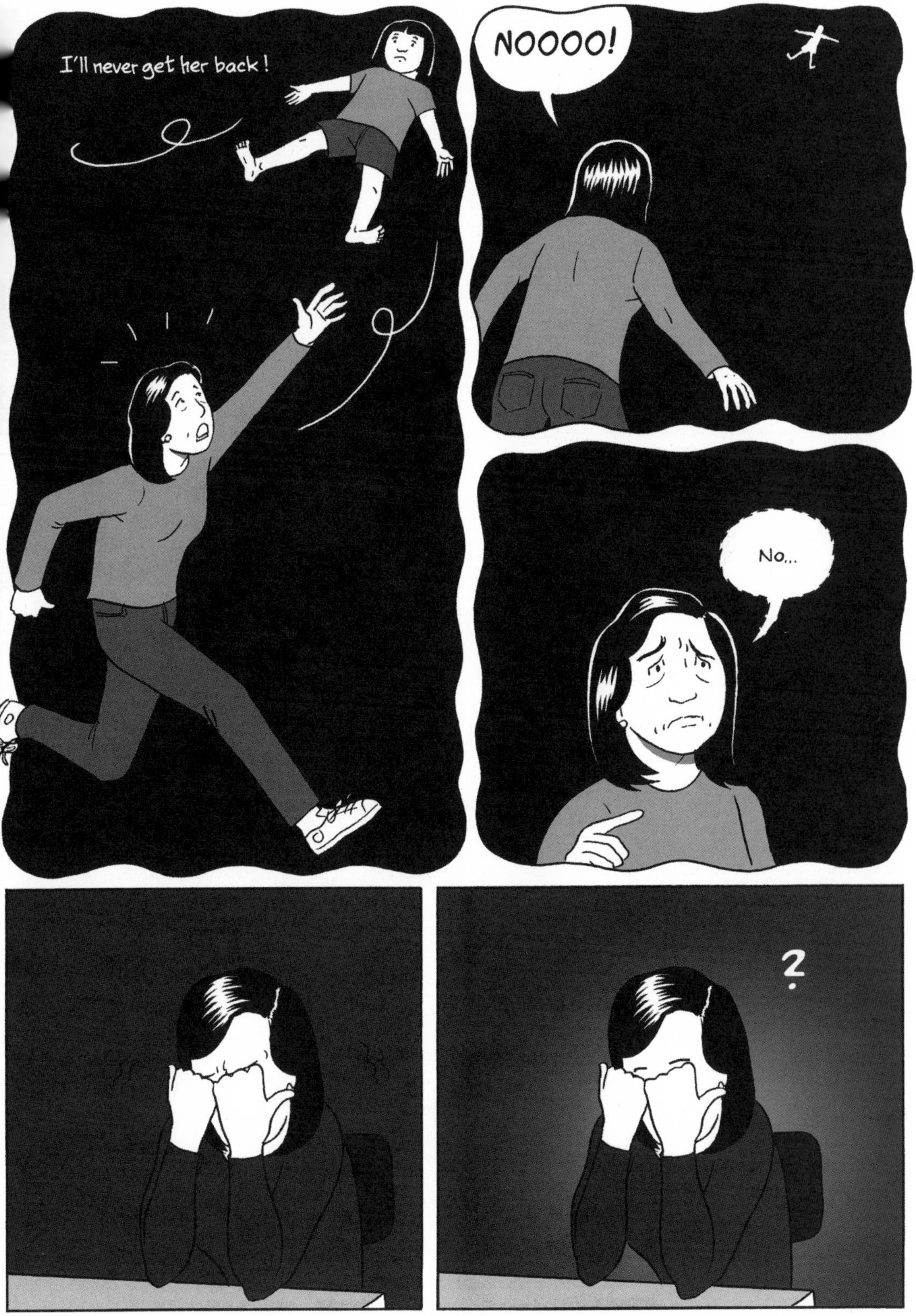
I'll never get her back!
NOOOO!
No...
?

And then it hits me.

It is my own death I have been mourning.

Ohhh! The feeling is incredible, like a great fog has been lifted.

Is that what I've been doing?

I am seeing clearly for the first time in a long time.

When confronted with death, you can deny it, keep fighting it. Try escaping it. Or you can face it.

In a strange way, only when you accept death can you bring back life.

There is a way to bring my dad and me back to life...

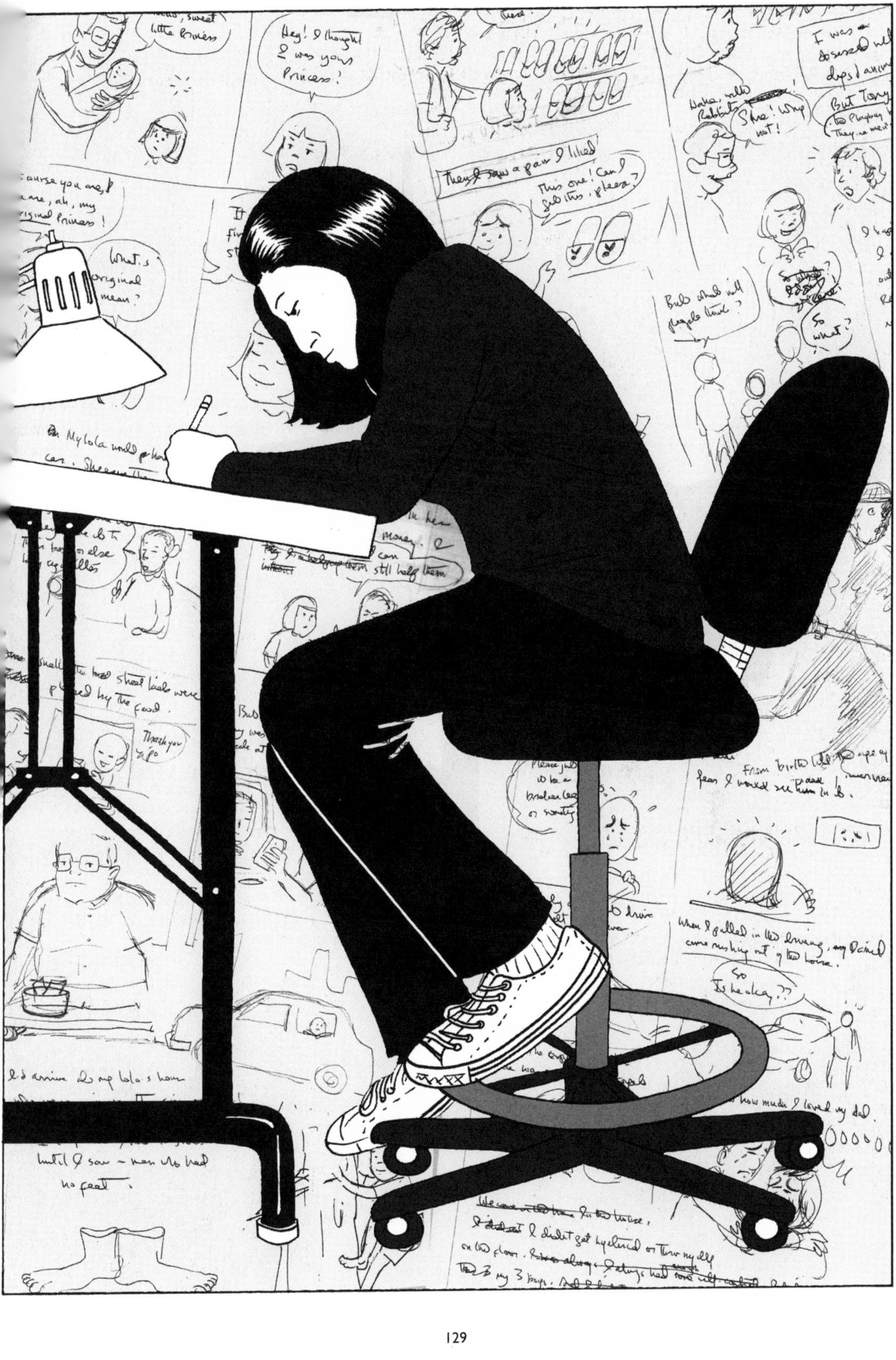

Hey! I thought I was your Princess!
What's original mean?
This one! Can I get this, please?
But what will people think?
So what?
So Is he okay??
until I saw men who had no feet.

When I finally look at the time, five hours have passed yet I hadn't noticed. I sit back and look in wonder at the piles of pages I have drawn.

It's like I've emerged from a dark cave I didn't even know I was in and am remembering how beautiful daylight is. I had forgotten.

The phone rings, jolting me out of my daze.

Hi Bunsen. Aren't you watching the Olympics? It's the final of men's hockey.

Huh? Oh yeah...

CLICK

Dan Boyle... Rick Nash... here comes Nash... SHOT! Stopped by Miller...

So? Any luck with your sketches?

Babe! I'm gonna do a graphic novel about my life growing up in the Philippines! I sketched all these stories about me and my dad! What do you think?

I think that's a great idea.... Hey, maybe you can use your revolution as a backdrop.

Oh my God, yeah! I haven't really thought it out, but yeah.

Back ahead now comes Sidney Crosby... Crosby tries to dance through... Miller guides it away to the corner... Crosby up with it there... punched along to Jerome Iginla... CROSBY SCORES!!!

SIDNEY CROSBY! The golden goal! And Canada has once again won the gold medal!

YESSS! YESSS!!!

Wow! Hello? Babe?

YEEHAH! WOOHOO! YAAAY!

Over the phone, I can hear Daniel and the kids celebrating Canada's victory. I hear Michael call Alec a dummy for farting, and Alec giggling in triumph. I can even hear Nicholas rolling his eyes. Then Mia comes on the phone.

I love you, Mommy!

All of a sudden, I miss them.

I love you too, sweetie.

≥CHAK≤

I thought I was lost. Or gone. But I'm still here.

I have always been here.

Gotta remember that.

Who am I?

I am myself.

I am me.

THE END

131

ACKNOWLEDGEMENTS

I am pleased to thank the following people whose interest and show of support in this project has been a great encouragement to me: Raymond Abejuela, Al Abdon, Torsten Adair, Haile Meregillano, Luc Bossé, Marygrace Burns, Helen Scott, Nena Zulueta Chauser, Jessica Gaytan, Bradley Walker, H.G. Aspera, Elin B. Mondejar, Chris Ross, William Halpin, Ryan DaCosta-McKenzie, Adrian Martinez (adrianmadethis.com), John Northey, Lennhoff Family, Rina Bautista, Samantha Rae Andico, Wally Hastings, Mary Spielman, Zoe Lewycky, E. Flinders-Jacobson, Michelle Y. Morris, Kathy Yan Li, Emilie Hanson, Mara Cabayan Aquino, Jose Eduardo Ang, Roxanne Amata Harris, Jeremy Tosch, Lily H., Liza Marie S. Erpelo, Gabriel Velarde and Knight of Words. And hello to Jason Isaacs.

My friends and relatives Mari Abello, Bimsy Mapa, Jerry Gobuyan, Norm Pige, Peachy Flores Trias (thank you!), Frederic Majeur, Anali Mapa Drilon, Jack and Sienna Scrocco (thanks Gianni), and to Gabrielle (thanks Sophie), Norma Torney-Bourgeois, Baba Tanada, Bernie Castellano and my favourite tito and tita, Noel and Lally Trinidad.

My fellow Kubies: Steve Dutro (who got behind this book very early on), Andy Smith, Todd Britton (who introduced me to Love and Rockets) and the great Ronald Jay "Krashboom" Krischbaum.

Those who have been enthusiastic from the beginning, JayJay Ferro, Manny Trinidad, Tisha Zarate-Caeg (fellow dog-lover) and Chinie Hidalgo-Diaz (fellow voracious reader and Remington Steele fan).

Tina Manalaysay (little sister!) and Suzette Montinola (fellow Alabum and star gazer): your generosity has truly humbled me.

Many thanks to Monina Mercado and her book *People Power: An Eyewitness History* which was an invaluable reference for my account of the EDSA Revolution.

Special thanks to Michel Rabagliati, creator of the great *bande-dessinée* series "Paul", who took time out of his busy schedule to look at my work, give me encouraging feedback, and most importantly write a blurb for my first book in print! Merci beaucoup, beaucoup, Michel.

To my terrific editor and publisher Andy Brown of Conundrum Press, for seeing something special in my story.

My dear Sisterhood of the Traveling Cousins: Nini Mapa, Tisa ("Cuthbert") Mapa-Roades, Anna (Manettish Creature) Mapa-Nad ("would you like some turkish delight?") and last but not least Claudine Arcenas-Abrenica who has been there for me since we were 1 and 2 years old.

My wonderful and kind in-laws Huguette and Arthur Shelton who welcomed me into their family and treated me like a daughter from the very beginning.

My siblings Miel Mapa-Sadwhani ("Bones"), Lisa Mapa-Sator ("Scotty"), Nikko Mapa ("Spock") and my big brother Tonton Mapa ("Manong") who has shown how proud he is of me and I am grateful.

My mom Marilyn Trinidad Mapa, who has been so supportive of this project. Although anything but a lurid tell-all, it can still be strange and uncomfortable reading about past events and real people as observed through someone else's eyes. Fortunately for me, my grandparents were journalists and so my mom understands the value and need in telling one's story. She has been the unsung hero in our family and I'm grateful I realized what an amazing, strong, selfless and caring person she has been for us all these years.

My sweet children and the best kids ever (especially since they read page 18 of this book and have stopped complaining so much — heh heh): Nicholas, Michael, Alec and Mia. I love you!!!!

Finally my husband and soulmate Daniel Shelton, yin to my yang, Bert to my Ernie, cream to my coffee, George to my Mary, and the best husband and father ever… not one panel of this book would have been possible without his relentless encouragement and support. Thanks Bunsen!

DISCOGRAPHY (1981-1986)

ABC
The Lexicon of Love (1982)
The Look of Love

AHA
Hunting High and Low (1985)
Take On Me / The Sun Always Shines On TV

Band Aid
Do They Know It's Christmas? (1984, Single)

Big Country
The Crossing (1983)
In a Big Country

Billy Idol
Rebel Yell (1983)
Eyes Without a Face / Flesh for Fantasy

The Cure
The Walk (1983)
Let's Go to Bed
The Head on the Door (1985)
In Between Days / Close to Me / A Night Like This

Dave Grusin
Mountain Dance (1980) - entire album
On Golden Pond (1982, Soundtrack)
Main Theme

David Benoit
Digits (1983)
Arthur's Theme / If I Could Reach Rainbows

David Bowie
Let's Dance (1983)
Modern Love / China Girl / Let's Dance

Depeche Mode
Speak and Spell (1981)
New Life / Just Can't Get Enough
A Broken Frame (1982)
My Secret Garden / See You
Construction Time Again (1983)
Love, In Itself / Everything Counts
Some Great Reward (1984)
*People Are People / Somebody / Master and
Servant / Blaspemous Rumours*

Duran Duran
Duran Duran (1981) - entire album
Rio (1982) - entire album
Seven And The Ragged Tiger (1983) - entire album

Earl Klugh
Crazy for You (1981)- entire album

Echo and the Bunnymen
Ocean Rain (1984)
The Killing Moon / Seven Seas
Echo and the Bunnymen (1986)
Lips Like Sugar

Eurythmics
Touch (1983)
Here Comes the Rain Again

Howard Jones
Dream into Action (1985)
Things Can Only Get Better / No One is to Blame

Joe Jackson
Night and Day (1982)
Steppin' Out / Breaking Us in Two

Level 42
World Machine (1985)
Something About You

Lotus Eaters
No Sense of Sin (1984)
First Picture of You

Madonna
Madonna (1983)
Borderline / Holiday / Everybody
Like a Virgin (1984)
Love Don't Live Here Anymore / Shoo-bee-doo
Crazy for You (1985, vision quest soundtrack)
True Blue (1986)
Open Your Heart / Live to Tell

Michael Jackson
Thriller (1982)
Human Nature / P.Y.T. (Pretty Young Thing)

Modern English
After the Snow (1982)
I Melt With You

New Order
Blue Monday (1983)
Thieves Like Us (1984)
Low-life (1985)
The Perfect Kiss
Brotherhood (1986)
Bizarre Love Triangle

Orchestral Maneuvers in the Dark
If You Leave (1986, Pretty in Pink soundtrack)

Pat Benatar
Live from Earth (1983)
Love is a Battlefield

Paul Young
No Parlez (1983)
Come Back and Stay

Pet Shop Boys
Please (1986)
West End Girls

Peter Gabriel
So (1986) - entire album

The Police
Ghost in the Machine (1981)
Spirits in the Material World / Every Little Thing She Does is Magic / Invisible Sun
Synchronicity (1983)
Walking in Your Footsteps / Synchronicity II / King of Pain
Don't Stand so Close to Me (1986, single)

Prefab Sprout
Steve McQueen (1985)
Appetite / When Love Breaks Down

Prince
When Doves Cry (1984, single)

Psychedelic Furs
Forever Now (1982)
Love My Way
Mirror Moves (1984)
The Ghost in You

Simple Minds
Don't You Forget About Me (single, 1985)

Spandau Ballet
True (1983)
True / Gold
Parade (1984)
Only When You Leave / I'll Fly for You / Round and Round

Sting
Dream of the Blue Turtles (1985) - entire album

The Smiths
The Smiths (1984)
This Charming Man / Hand in Glove
Hatful of Hollow (1984)
William, It Was Really Nothing / These Things Take Time / Heaven Knows I'm Miserable Now / This Night Has Opened My Eyes / Girl Afraid / Please, Please, Please Let Me Get What I Want
Meat is Murder (1985)
That Joke Isn't Funny Anymore / How Soon Is Now?
The Queen is Dead (1986) - entire album

Talk, Talk
It's My Life (1984)
It's My Life

Tears for Fears
The Hurting (1983)
Mad World / Suffer the Children / Start of the Breakdown
Songs from the Big Chair (1985)
The Working Hour / Everybody Wants to Rule the World / Head over Heels

Thompson Twins
Into the Gap (1984)
Doctor! Doctor! / Hold Me Now / Who Can Stop the Rain

Tina Turner
Mad Max Beyond Thunderdome (1985, soundtrack)
We Don't Need Another Hero

U2
Under a Blood Red Sky (1983)
Sunday Bloody Sunday / New Year's Day
The Unforgettable Fire (1984)
A Sort of Homecoming / Pride (In the Name of Love) / Bad

Ultravox
Monument (1983, soundtrack)
Reap the Wild Wind
Lament (1984)
Dancing with Tears in My Eyes